Buildings for Hospitality

Principles of Care and Design for Accommodation Managers

Jane and Richard Fellows

 LONGMAN

Addison Wesley Longman Limited
Edinburgh Gate, Harlow
Essex CM20 2JE
England

and Associated Companies throughout the World

First published in Great Britain in 1990

Reprinted 1996
Third impression Addison Wesley Longman Limited 1998

ISBN 0 582 36848 0

British Library Cataloguing-in-Publication Data
A catalogue record for this book is
available from the British Library.

Library of Congress Cataloging-in-Publication Data
A catalog entry for this title is
available from the Library of Congress.

Set by
Produced through Longman Malaysia, PP

Contents

Acknowledgements

The preparation of this book would not have been possible without the help of the following people and organisations:

Mr G Halstead
British Standards Institute
Fearnville Sports Centre, Leeds
Health and Safety Commission
Hotel and Catering Training Company
Leeds City Council, Department of Leisure Services
Rentokil Ltd
Royal Institute of British Architects
The Sports Council

Sm98009410
b/99
£21-99

UXY
(Fel)

Buildings for Hospitality
Principles of Care and Design
for Accommodation Managers

058 236 8480

a. Basic
   shelter

b. Environmental
   modification

c. Privacy &
   security

Fig 1.1 Building enclosure: the basic functions

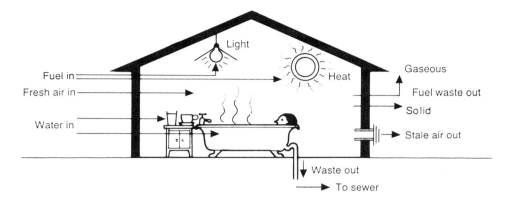

Fig 1.2 Basic services in a small building

electricity to such an extent that it is scarcely able to function on any level if the supply fails.

The design and operation of these services systems is just one factor in the creation of the built environment, which has become increasingly complex as the opportunities presented by advancing technology have been realised, and as standards and expectations have risen. Building design is, therefore, the net outcome of many pressures. Chapter 2 looks at design considerations and the process of design. Structural and construction matters are discussed in Chapter 3 and services in Chapters 4, 5 and 6.

Participants in building design, control and maintenance

The complex tasks connected with the design, construction, operation and maintenance of buildings are the responsibility of a variety of individuals. Some of these may be classed as creators and enablers, others as operators of controls and safeguards. Anyone involved with the running of premises is bound to come into contact with at least some of these people during the course of his or her work.

1 Creators, enablers and maintainers

This category includes the architect and other design professionals, the surveyor, the structural engineer and the services engineer.

Building contractors, tradespeople and technical specialists undertake the physical realisation of decisions made at a professional level.

The roles must now be considered separately.

a The architect

The architect is the person traditionally charged with an overview of the whole process of building design and construction. This role has become increasingly complex and difficult to fulfil in recent years. Of course, during the creation of a large, modern building other professionals who have specialised knowledge are involved.

An architect can be employed in the production of a new building, extensions to an existing building or any one of a number of processes concerned with old buildlings, such as rehabilitation. In the case of 'new build', a 'full service' may be offered whereby the architect is concerned with both the design and the supervision of construction. Typically, the architect acts as an agent for the client, and as an intermediary between the client and the building contractor. The tasks that an architect may undertake, and the processes of design and construction are considered in more depth in Chapter 2.

The word 'architect' is protected by law and only properly qualified persons may use it. It normally takes a minimum of seven years to qualify, after which an applicant may register with the Architect's Registration Council of the UK. However, there is no bar to anyone who wishes to practise building design, and unqualified individuals may be found describing themselves as 'architectural designers' or even 'architectural consultants'.

It is important to realise that a large part of the architect's training concerns brief formulation. At the outset the client may have rigid ideas about the kind of building that is required, but the architect can often produce a variety of design possibilities. A clear brief can then be formulated from which a more successful building will result.

Despite the comprehensive nature of the architect's services it may be desirable to employ other professionals if the work in hand is on a large scale or is complex.

b The quantity surveyor

The quantity surveyor produces *Bills of Quantities* for larger projects showing the amount, type and quality of building work to be produced. From this, cost estimates can be made. Advice on cost control and contract type is given before work begins. Complicated contracts and variations in management and construction processes now often require the quantity surveyor's more active participation. Completed work will be measured as the job proceeds.

c The building surveyor

A building surveyor usually advises where an existing property is to be purchased or altered and the state of the building needs to be ascertained. Some specialised surveyors can offer financial advice about building values and market prices, and provide consultancy services on feasibility. The surveyor may also prepare specifications and inspect new work.

d The structural engineer

The structural engineer works with the architect to design and calculate the type and layout of structural members, their sizes and the materials to be used.

e The services engineer

> The services engineer advises on the creation of environmental conditions within the building, and evolves a services strategy to meet these conditions. Engineers concerned with heating, ventilation, lighting, acoustics and a whole host of services systems come under this heading.
>
> All of the above belong to professional institutions and have to abide by their codes of conduct. Their task is to advise impartially and without commercial bias. The client may, however, decide to use a 'package deal'. In this case a construction company employing its own architects and engineers will undertake design and construction. There are advantages and disadvantages to this method which are discussed in Chapter 2.

f The interior designer

> The interior designer also has an important role, particularly in the case of hotel, restaurant and public house schemes. Given a building shell, the designer can produce creative themes which are considered to be important in generating custom in commercial premises. Such projects are subject to the vagaries of fashion. The designer may also advise on decoration and finishes in existing buildings.

g The general contractor

> The general contractor usually handles building construction. The contractor undertakes to control and organise the works and to employ sub-contractors, some of whom may have been nominated by the architect, for specialised tasks. The employer's and the architect's relationship with the contractor are further outlined in Chapter 2.
>
> In some specialised contracts the management and construction functions are separated.

2 Operators of controls and safeguards

> This category includes planning officers, building inspectors, fire officers, factories inspectors, public health inspectors and crime prevention officers. These publicly employed officials ensure that any activity connected with public buildings is conducted in a manner that safeguards the individual and society at large. Those who operate controls and safeguards are involved before, during and after construction. Generally speaking, they apply and enforce legislation to make sure that the public interest is not harmed.

a The planning officer

> The planning officer is an employee of the local council. He or she has to implement local planning policy: what type and size of building is allowed to go where, for instance. The planning officer is also concerned with details of the proposed building's appearance, and should be consulted before any

building works are instituted, as in most cases planning permission will be required. The planning officer can order the removal of any building erected without permission, when such permission was required.

Planning legislation is more fully dealt with in Chapter 2.

b The building control officer (building inspector)

The building control officer is also employed by the local authority to ensure that any new building construction conforms to the Building Regulations. The Building Regulations, a statutory instrument, are long and involved and cover a whole range of subjects concerning environmental and constructional standards to ensure safety and health. (*See* Chapter 2.)

Generally, before any new building works are commenced, appropriate drawings must be submitted both to the planning officer and building inspector, and approvals must be obtained.

c The fire officer

The fire officer is often consulted by the architect during the process of building design. The fire officer is particularly interested in means of escape from buildings during fire and safeguarding the public from the effects of fire and smoke when inside the buildings. For this reason the fire officer makes sure that legislation related to public buildings and 'places of entertainment and resort' is strictly enforced. Similarly, members of the *Factories Inspectorate* enforce Health and Safety at Work Act regulations to ensure that staff are safeguarded.

d The environmental health officer

The environmental health officer is concerned with health and hygiene in places where food is prepared for public consumption.

e The crime prevention officer

The crime prevention officer is attached to the local police force, and acts in an advisory capacity on security issues and other matters associated with crime avoidance.

It may be felt that the officials listed above impose too many restrictions, but it must be remembered that by and large their remit is to ensure the public good. (Further information on legislative issues is contained in Chapter 2.)

Communications

1 Drawings

In dealing with professionals, contractors, tradesmen and officials, drawings are often used as the primary means of communication. It is useful to be able to understand them and the conventions employed, and to realise their advantages and limitations.

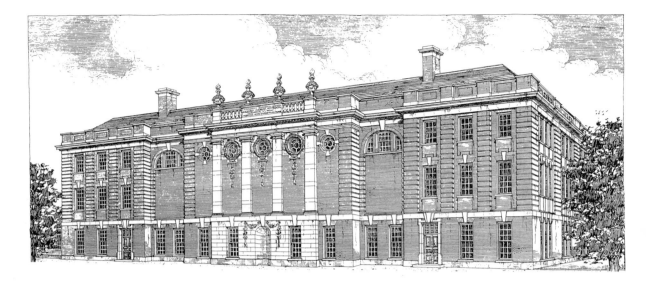

Fig 1.3 Perspective view of the exterior of a building

Non-specialised drawings are used by architects and designers to show clients what projected buildings will look like when complete. Such drawings often take the form of 'perspectives' of the interior or exterior of the building which attempt to show the final scheme as realistically as possible. However, the temptation is to present a very rosy picture, to exaggerate certain features and to show the work in its most favourable light.

Alternatively, a scale model may be produced. This is an expensive but very effective means of communication. Taken one stage further, the model can be photographed and a 'montage' prepared, together with photographs of the site, showing the new building in existing surroundings. In addition, with the aid of special camera attachments a video tape can be made, giving impressions of internal spaces, providing that the original model is sufficiently detailed. Similar images may be computer-generated.

Such efforts are of only passing interest, however, to the specialist, and technical drawings have to be prepared for the following purposes:

- Communication within the professional team (architects, quantity surveyors, engineers).
- Communication with statutory authorities and utilities (electricity, water, gas, highways).
- Communication with bodies exercising legal control (building control and planning).
- Communication with the general contractor, sub-contractors and tradesmen.
- Communication with the maintenance manager.

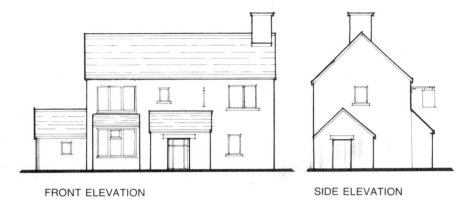

FRONT ELEVATION   SIDE ELEVATION

Fig 1.4 Front and side elevations

In all of these cases the technical drawings which are used follow certain conventions and do not attempt to represent a 'real' view. Anyone concerned with the maintenance, security, running or care of buildings should have practice in 'reading' such drawings and interpreting their meaning.

The type of drawing most commonly found is the 'orthographic' projection. This represents buildings as plans, sections and elevations, and in all cases a view is taken as though it is perpendicular to the plane of the building (*see* Figs 1.4, 1.5 and 1.6).

Elevations show side views of the building, but when reading drawings care should be taken because representations are hypothetical, and the effects of perspective which would be seen in real life are eliminated (*see* Fig 1.4).

Sections show vertical slices through the building (*see* Fig 1.5).

Plans are horizontal sections and show horizontal slices through the building (*see* Fig 1.6).

All of these drawings help the observer to build up a picture of the layout of the building and the organisation of spaces. Orthographic projection can

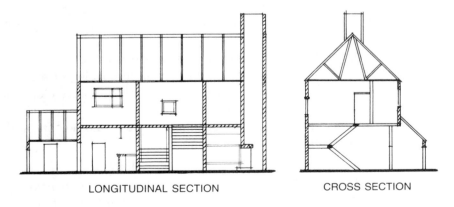

LONGITUDINAL SECTION   CROSS SECTION

Fig 1.5 Longitudinal and cross sections

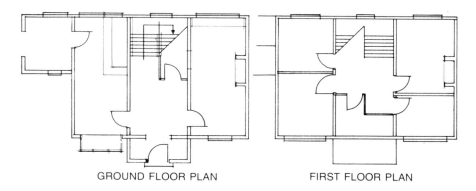

GROUND FLOOR PLAN   FIRST FLOOR PLAN

Fig 1.6   Ground floor and first floor plans

easily be drawn to scale and it is therefore possible to see the relative proportions and sizes of spaces, and in some cases to 'scale off' drawings to obtain dimensions (though it is not good practice to do this in building construction, where dimensions written on the drawings should be used).

'Isometric' and 'axonometric' drawings are three-dimensional views drawn to scale, but, again, they are not 'realistic' representations. They are used mainly where they are easier to understand than an orthographic drawing, for instance to show different heights of sections of a building, or layouts on several floors.

2   Scale

It is necessary to understand scale because it is impracticable to draw whole buildings full size! A scale is therefore used which shows everything in proportion, but much smaller than in real life. If a scale of 1:100 is employed, for instance, a wall 25m long will be represented by a line 25/100m long, i.e. 250mm. Detailed parts of buildings may be shown at a larger scale. Those in common use are:

1:1250	Site plan, showing building in location.
1:500	Block plan showing the position of the building relative to the site.
1:200; 1:100	General layout of a largish building.
1:50	General layout of a smallish building or room layout.
1:20	Detailed constructional sections, plans etc, showing building elements and materials.
1:10; 1:5; 1:2 and full size (FS)	Intricate constructional details, e.g. joinery work, junctions within the building.

Buildings in Britain are now designed in metric dimensions and when these are shown in figures on drawings it must be remembered that the European SI system (Système Internationale d'Unités) is used. For instance, 3,127 is

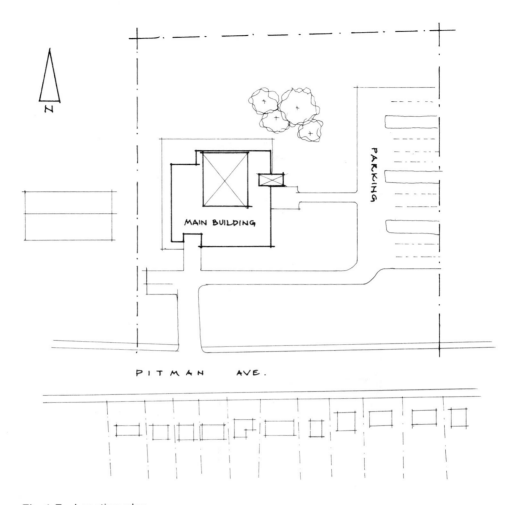

Fig 1.7 Location plan

three metres and one hundred and twenty-seven millimetres. (Centimetres are not used, except of course on the Continent where the system originated.)

Older drawings will probably be in imperial units, i.e. feet and inches. In this case scales employed are usually:

⅛″ to 1 foot (1:96); ¼″ to 1 foot (1:48); ½″ to 1 foot (1:24); 1″ to 1 foot (1:12); ½FS and FS.

Standard layout drawings usually form the base for representing other information, i.e. the line of air handling ducts; layout of sprinkler systems; positioning of furniture or plant.

Before, and during the building process many drawings are produced. Copies of the most relevant should be kept for record purposes, together with instructions relating to mechanical and electrical services. When alterations occur copies of drawings relating to these should also be added to records.

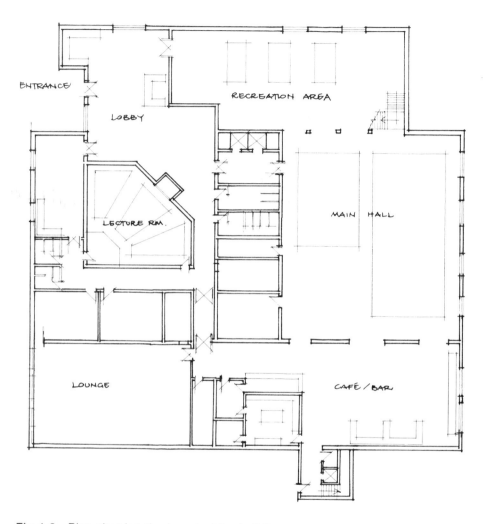

Fig 1.8   Plan showing the layout of the building

Drawings produced on computers are especially useful, as alterations can easily be made throughout whole sets of drawings.

There is a tendency to think that, once built, the building requires no further 'servicing' and the fabric is left until failure occurs. However, buildings must be properly maintained. Several types of flat roof, for instance, have a strictly limited life. Painting of timber and metalwork may have to be arranged regularly, and any consequences of frost action or shrinkage should be noted. This work is in addition to maintenance of mechanical services. A

Organisation and space

The basis of space allocation and planning at the smallest scale is to do with 'anthropometrics', the shape, proportion and size of the human body, and 'ergonomics', the study of work and movement (*see* Fig 2.1).

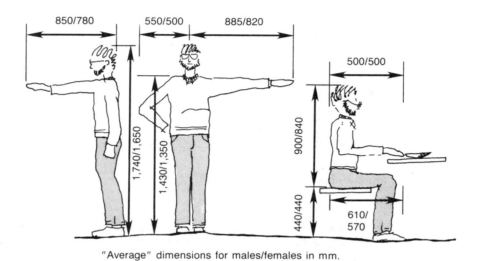

"Average" dimensions for males/females in mm.

Fig 2.1 Typical anthropometric considerations

Neither ergonomics nor anthropometrics can give exact answers. People's body sizes vary greatly amongst the adult population, not to mention children. In theory, common objects or layouts are designed around average sizes and those people falling outside the norm have to put up with the disadvantages of being too big, too small or disabled (see end of this chapter). Examples of objects and layouts adjusted to the norm include worktop heights, reach heights for cupboards, space behind tables for sitting and rising, widths of doors and corridors and widths of entrances and exits (although the latter are modified by fire regulations).

Small-scale planning always has to bear these physical sizes in mind, but there is an additional factor. This is organisation, based on an understanding of how a job is to be done and the relationships required between individual operations. For example, when designing a bedroom layout, allowance has to be made for space to get in and out of the bed and to make it, and for the proximity of the bedside shelf or table, the relationship of bed space to washing, WC facilities and clothes storage, and the size of dressing area required. All of these factors are combined in the three-dimensional problem of organising a bedroom. Very many more are involved in its comprehensive design, and this is just one of the spaces within a building.

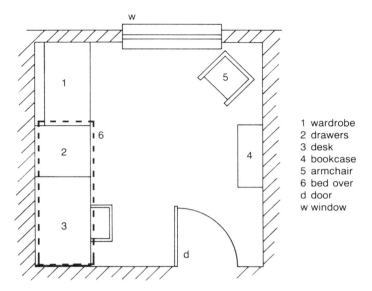

1 wardrobe
2 drawers
3 desk
4 bookcase
5 armchair
6 bed over
d door
w window

Fig 2.2 Plan of a study bedroom

Standard dimensions can be used, for example, for a student hostel bedroom (*see* Fig 2.2). This approach is handy when working out requirements for a bedroom extension. It is a good, approximate way of totting up floor areas to estimate space and costs, but it can lead to a reactive, rather than progressive, response and a blindness to novel solutions. A problem is that, typically, planning and organisational diagrams are two dimensional and in the horizontal plane.

It will be noted that although Fig 2.2 purports to be the plan of a study bedroom, the bed is absent. This is because it is positioned over the desk and drawers, as shown by the dotted line, but does not appear on the ground plan. This example illustrates the shortcoming of two-dimensional planning and the problem of plan reading (*see* Chapter 1).

Space standards

Specialist books are available which give typical dimensions for a whole range of different buildings and purposes. In theory, each case may be unique, but reference to standard works is a convenient way of determining the amount of space needed for everyday activities. The accommodation manager could consider producing a personal catalogue of relevant examples of space standards pertinent to his or her particular situation.

Larger-scale planning may be approached initially from a diagrammatic point of view. Matrices can be used to show relationships, but most popular is the bubble diagram (*see* Fig 2.3). No definite scale or shape is given to areas or activities but their relationship is shown. The connecting lines can

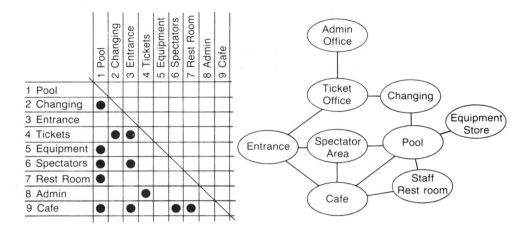

Fig 2.3   Matrix and 'bubble diagram', showing relationships, for a small swimming pool

be given different colours or strengths to indicate the kind of relationship. It does not always mean that one area must be next door to another, or indeed that there should be personal access: sometimes a telephone or computer link might be adequate. However, it does allow clear thought to be concentrated on relationships. A common mistake is to convert the bubble diagram to a rudimentary plan by drawing the spaces to scale and using the proximities and links represented on the diagram. However, while this can serve as a guide for those trying to work out areas and rough costs, or to determine whether a site is large enough to contain new accommodation, it still does not produce a design.

A design integrates a number of complex factors from space standards to structure and from physical environment to maintenance, brought together in a way that will satisfy physical, financial, legal and aesthetic criteria.

Architectural character

The character of a building is important in various ways: it can be used, for instance, to provide the theme for a leisure or accommodation operation, or, more prosaically, it can define and limit the uses to which the building can be put and how it can be altered. It is not only worth respecting a building's character in terms of safeguarding an asset, but it should be remembered that most buildings exist in the public domain and that the owners have a duty to their fellow citizens when considering changes to a building's appearance or function.

Although the term 'character' seems difficult to define, it may be examined briefly under a number of headings which can provide a helpful checklist to use when attempting to describe a building.

1   Structure and construction

The way in which the building is built is one of the chief determining factors of character. Most buildings are either of 'loadbearing' or 'framed' structure (these are fully discussed in Chapter 3). Framed buildings generally appear to be light, with panels or glazing fixed to a timber, steel or concrete frame. Loadbearing structures look heavy and solid, with large areas of brick or stone construction and relatively small areas of windows and doors.

The method of construction also affects the building's appearance. It is possible, for instance, to emphasise the thickness of a wall by the position of door and window frames within its width. A roof which overhangs with wide eaves gives quite a different effect to one which stops flush with the wall of the building.

2   Materials

The materials from which the building 'envelope' is constructed have an obvious effect upon character. A building clad in glass sheets, for instance, has a slick, rather hard, glossy character compared with a similar building clad in brick which may look warm, human and 'friendly'.

3   Scale

Scale and size are not the same thing. Quite a small building can have a big 'scale' and vice versa (*see* Fig 2.4). The easiest way to think of scale is in relation to human beings. Small-scale buildings respond to the body in the same way an ordinary house does: the door is just a little bigger than the minimum size of gap you need to go through, and window openings, too, are related to the size of the body. In large-scale buildings, all the elements which are used to judge the size of the building are big. Doors may be of superhuman size or huge chunks of stone may be used instead of brick; big, impressive elements constitute the building, rather than lots of small ones.

4   Proportion

'Proportion' is a frequently misused word. Proportion reflects the relationship between different elements of a building or its components. For example, it may concern the width to height ratio of a window or door frame *or* the relationship of window(s) and door(s) to the front of a building as a whole. It could also refer to the plan dimensions of a space relative to its height.

It is generally supposed that architecture deriving from classical (i.e. Greek) origins shows the most sophisticated and subtle regard for proportion.

5 Massing

This word describes the way in which chunks of the building are disposed next to each other. The building may be broken up and fragmented, or it could read as one huge block or several fairly massive chunks lumped together.

6 Detail and features

Many non-specialists remember a building not by its overall massing, disposition or structure, but by details and applied features. These can give distinction to a building and even generate a theme. *Details* usually arise out of construction: the details of window sills and lintels, the picking out of 'quoin' stones on corners, the brackets which support the eaves.

Features may be applied, for instance, works of art such as statuary, sculpture, murals and friezes frequently form part of older buildings. They can even have practical use, like a clock or lantern. These are particularly important in urban buildings – 'meet me under the clock'.

7 Form and space

Building form is often dictated by planning demands, and subsequently the disposition of spaces, growing out of organisational criteria. 'Deep plan' buildings are found where large, uninterrupted spaces are required, for example a sports hall or theatre auditorium. These large single cells are surrounded by smaller-scale subservient accommodation, such as foyers, lobbies and changing facilities. 'Narrow plan' additive buildings, formed from multiple small cells, arise out of the need for small, repetitive spaces. An example may be a hall of residence or the accommodation wing of an hotel.

Both types have implications in terms of structure and servicing as well as character. The first type leads to a dominating form sitting prominently on its site, the second to a more 'elastic' form which can enclose external space.

8 Style

Style results from many of the aspects of built form discussed above, plus other important factors which have acted to shape buildings at various periods during history. For example, the medieval 'Gothic' style which characterises some of our churches results from the materials used, the current technology for spanning space, the medieval view of life, and the amount of time and money available for building: all these combined to form the Gothic style. In the eighteenth century, or Georgian period, technology had not particularly advanced, but although these buildings are fairly rudimentary structurally, the main aspect of the style concerns the social climate in the 'Age of Reason', which is reflected in the cool, well-proportioned façades and interiors.

Bank of England Branch, Liverpool

Fig 2.4   A small building with a large scale and (opposite) a large building keeping to a smaller, domestic scale

Newnham College, Cambridge

Most importantly, 'style' should not be thought of in terms of a catalogue of 'add-on' details. Any attempts to change a building's style in such a way may produce laughable results.

Having looked at character it should be possible to think in terms of the building's use, maintenance and possible change in a more considered light. For example, if extending a large Victorian house, currently used as an hotel or hostel, to provide a suite of conference rooms, a variety of designs may be produced. These will probably conform to two main approaches:

- *Fitting in with the existing building*, using similar materials and form and reflecting the massive, heavy quality of the building. Forms are 'articulated', split up and angular. Decoration and sculpture are both present. The result could be an attempt to reproduce Victorian design or a modern interpretation using current materials and techniques.
- *Contrast*, by letting the modern extension 'speak' and using lightweight structures and modern cladding materials. In short, a contrast between the new with the old, but not in a discordant way.

By considering the character of the building, the chief asset will be enhanced in value as will the business itself and the whole neighbourhood.

The process of change

Strategies for decision making

If change to the building is necessary, it is important that clear thought is given to new requirements through an assessment of the character and potential of the existing accommodation. The financial implications and overall viability of the project must also be considered. Significant questions may include whether:

- it is cheaper to modify the existing building or to provide totally new accommodation
- the service areas of the building will cope with alterations and additions
- the existing building will be difficult to modify: will its form readily admit change; would it be better to completely reorganise the existing building rather than extend it?

Leasing of additional accommodation may also be an alternative. Good professional advice taken at this stage may well pay for itself in the long term.

If change is inevitable, then it will generally fall into one of four categories:

- refurbishing and redecorating
- reorganisation
- extension
- the production of a completely new building.

As has been indicated, many considerations are important before a decision can be taken, but underlying all − in most cases − is the question of finance. Initially, capital outlay is critical, but so, also, are the recurring costs associated with running and maintenance. A completely new building or major extension may cost more initially, but operationally the building may be superior to an extended existing building, and ongoing costs will be saved. A new low-maintenance building should be cheaper to keep in good order than an older one where materials are deteriorating and where the design includes a large number of joints and junctions which could decay. On the other hand, high capital outlay invariably involves borrowing, and interest repayments may cancel out all the financial advantages of a new structure (*see* Chapter 8, life cycle costing).

In the case of major extensions or new buildings, the site has to be considered. In urban locations it is quite likely that the only way to extend is to build upwards, therefore the choice is either a vertical extension or relocation to a larger site elsewhere. Thought must be given to site potential; factors such as orientation, views out of buildings, and views of buildings from on- and off-site should be assessed. Aside from aesthetic considerations, a commercial establishment may be able to advertise its presence with a building that at once attracts attention, and, through its style, conveys the character of the institution to the passer-by.

Any course of action should not be undertaken lightly. A chart indicating how the building fits into future plans, both financial and operational, and the likely expected maintenance, alterations and additions could be a suitable method of clarifying thought on this topic. A sobering exercise is to cost out the building in terms of construction, maintenance and running costs per square metre and set these against income that must be generated to cover these costs.

The process of design and building

The accommodation manager should understand the various processes involved in new building work. The manager may become a member of the team responsible for the briefing stage of the process, and the specification of performance levels.

For new building work certain courses of action may be followed:

- employ a designer (usually an architect) to design the building and supervise its construction
- approach a building firm who will offer a 'package deal'
- buy or rent 'off the peg' ready-made lightweight structures.

This describes the options somewhat crudely, but provides basic categories into which they fall. There are advantages and disadvantages to each of these courses of action which will be discussed briefly, though the first option will later be considered at length.

1 Employing a designer

Advantages

- It allows a direct response to particular requirements, rather like having a tailor-made suit.
- It allows discussion about requirements to take place with specialists so that it is easier to build up a brief and obtain satisfactory results.
- It allows competitive tendering amongst builders so that the best financial deal is obtained.
- The architect acts as his or her client's agent, but also stands between contractor and client to ensure fair dealing by both parties.
- The standard of work is monitored.

Disadvantages

- There may be a clash of personalities between architect and employer.
- The employer may feel that the architect's priorities and design ideology obscure what is really required.

■ It can be a laborious process, because many people are involved. It is not like the purchase of equipment.

2 Employing a building firm for a 'package deal'

Advantages

■ It is a quick and simple response with no need for tendering between the design and building process. The builder may design to optimise the construction method with which he is most familiar so that there could be fewer problems.
■ All is contained in one package. Contact is with one concern, rather than paying architect's fees, structural engineer's fees, quantity surveyor's fees and contractor's fees. There are fewer people involved in the equation.

Disadvantages

■ The range of design possibilities may be limited. The builder may want to do what he does best or what is easier, despite what may really be possible.
■ There is no specialist outside the process to represent the client's interest.

3 Buying or renting a ready-made structure

Advantages

■ Essentially it is no more difficult than buying or hiring other pieces of equipment although planning permission is usually required if the building is to be permanent.

Disadvantages

■ There is a limited range of possibilities and lack of flexibility.
■ It may not be aesthetically suitable for the client, his customers *or* the planning authorities.
■ Environmental and energy standards may be poor, e.g. bad lighting, high heat loss, crude internal qualities.
■ There may be poor durability. (Of course, certain manufacturers will have higher standards than others.)

The last option is probably the best for solving very short-term problems, such as the need for temporary accommodation.

It should be remembered in the case of the first options that the building being produced is probably a 'one-off', something especially designed for a particular function on a particular site. It is therefore liable to problems somewhere along the line which may even arise after construction.

Stages of design and building work

In order to understand the process of design and construction it is useful to consider what happens when an architect is appointed to undertake design and supervision. The 'client' may be the building owner or, for operational purposes, a management employee or the spokesman of a team set up to produce a brief for the new building. The architect can be chosen by approaching the Royal Institute of British Architects for advice, by personal recommendation, or by noting successful examples of the kind of work anticipated.

The stages of work are included in material published by the RIBA to act as a guide for client and architect. These stages are summarised below, and are split into 'preliminary' and 'basic' services. Even if a different system is to be used, e.g. the DSS's Capricode for health service buildings, it is a useful indication of the process.

1 Preliminaries

Inception Discussion takes place about the nature of the client's requirements, timescale of work and financial limits. The type of agreement with the architect and the possible need for involvement of other professionals is also discussed. Information about the proposed site is transmitted and if there are alternatives they may be evaluated.

Feasibility and alternatives The extent of work on this particular site allowed by financial constraints is considered; the architect will advise whether building regulations approval and planning permission are required.

2 Basics

After agreement on preliminaries, the architect can be instructed to produce:

a Outline proposals

An approximate cost can be worked out, e.g. on a unit basis, in conjunction with other consultants if necessary.

b Scheme design

This is produced once the outline proposals have been considered and agreed. The client should agree on spatial organisation and appearance, and the architect can produce models and drawings which show what the building will be like (*see* Chapter 1). Drawings for planning approval can be prepared once the client is satisfied with the scheme.

c Detail design

Decisions are then made on the best way of constructing the building and the nature of materials and finishes. This is a good time for client input on details that are so important in day-to-day running.

If the client's detailed approval is sought at this stage, the architect can then submit a design for building regulations approval, and a more accurate idea of cost can be worked out. It is *not* a good idea to make alterations after this stage, but if the working relationship with the architect has been good then it should not be necessary.

d Production drawings

The architect can now go ahead and produce drawings which communicate with the building contractor and other specialists. These are not intended for client use.

At this stage a *specification* can be written, setting out standards of materials, components and work. Where a largish or fairly complicated building is concerned, a *bill of quantities* can be produced by the quantity surveyor, liaising with the architect, whose appointment and employment by the client will already have been suggested.

Bills of quantity can take various forms and describe all work to be done by division into trades or operations. Prepared bills of quantities can be sent out to selected building contractors by the architect and tendering procedures are entered into, whereby the bills are priced by the builders. All *tenders* have to be submitted by a certain time on a certain day and the builder can then be chosen on the basis of price. (It should be noted that there are several variations and options in terms of project management and contract other than this traditional method, such as fast-track operations.)

However the new work is to be undertaken, some kind of *contract* must exist between the employer and the building contractor. There are standard forms of contract in existence, the most popular of which are issued by the Joint Contracts Tribunal (JCT) and the Association of Consultant Architects (ACA).

Standard JCT contract forms cover a range of typical situations from the traditional case where an architect is employed and a lump sum contract is agreed (JCT 80), through to the form with contractor's design. There is a form of agreement for minor works which can be useful for small-scale extensions. Careful consideration should be given to the type of contract which is most suitable depending on the size of work involved, the timescale, and any operational problems envisaged.

Contracts must be signed with the chosen contractor and then the process of organising the running of the project can be started. The architect must administer the contract and ensure that both parties are maintaining their legal responsibilities. Site inspections are undertaken to ensure that the building is built in accordance with contract drawings; provision is made so that the contractor is paid as agreed and that the effects of any variations or changes during the building process are monitored and reported upon to the client.

When the building work is 'practically completed' certificates of *completion* may be signed and the procedure for payment of monies undertaken. When work is complete, there is a defects liability period, during which faults must be made good by the contractor. A maintenance guide for building operators and record drawings are prepared.

These services are provided by architects when they are involved in the 'job' from start to finish. It may be that only 'partial services' are called for, such as the early design stages. There are a whole range of additional tasks that architects can provide which may be of value, for instance in the choice of sites or buildings and negotiations with planners. The employer should agree the type and method of fee payment with the architect at a preliminary stage. The RIBA produces a booklet as a guide to architects' clients which the architect can make available.

Services normally provided by consultants, rather than architects, on more complex projects include: quantity surveying, structural engineering, mechanical engineering, landscape architecture and civil engineering.

The complexity of the building process is apparent, even from the somewhat crude outline here. Before embarking on a project it is important to recognise the desirability of making clear decisions and communicating in a straightforward, unambiguous manner, given the number of different individuals and variables involved.

3 Fees

Architects' fees are 'recommended' by the professional institution (RIBA) but are not mandatory. Fees may be paid as a percentage of the construction cost, or based on time expended, or a lump sum. For projects valued between £20 000 and £5 000 000 a percentage is charged, depending on the cost and complexity of the scheme. A large storage shed, for instance, would merit a much lower percentage than a luxury hotel.

Legislation

One of the main problems which is present in the process of design and building is the need to cope with legislation as it applies to the planning, construction and operation of a building. Such legislation is usually there to protect the general public. Most dominant in the process are the twin consents necessary for almost all new development of any size: planning permission and building regulations approval.

1 Planning legislation

This dates in its present form from the 1947 Town and Country Planning Act (now the 1971 Act), the purpose of which was to ensure control over the use of land and provision of appropriate development. It respected the notion of broad zoning of land for various uses in order to avoid what were considered to be the unhealthy and unpleasant mixtures of housing and industry which had arisen during the Industrial Revolution. This idea has been largely abandoned, but the local authority, in this case the district council, acting through the planning officer under the powers conferred on it by section 107 of the 1972 Local Government Act, is concerned with the kind of development proposed. Its 'local plan' will have been prepared to establish principles within its area. It may wish to encourage new development in some areas and discourage it in others. It may have identified a place of 'environmental amenity' – say a riverside walk – where recreational and refreshment facilities, suitably designed, would be allowed, but little else.

The local authority, therefore, has control over what goes on, and where. There are also aesthetic considerations, and the planning officer requires a description of the proposed design so that its suitability, relative to the appearance of its surroundings, can be checked.

The architect can prepare the necessary forms and drawings for planning application. Outline consent can be granted for the size and type of development envisaged, in other words, whether the proposal is acceptable in principle to the planning officer and the authority. Detailed consent will involve inspection of drawings which show the building design in some detail, with notes as to materials and finishes.

A number of factors affect the planning officer's attitude, from adequacy of car parking provision through to the colour of brickwork. The officer then makes a recommendation to the democratically-elected council for its decision. Failure to comply with the council's decision can lead to drastic measures such as the demolition of buildings constructed without permission. Appeals against planning decisions can be made to the Secretary of State for the Environment.

'Listed' buldings – buildings of special architectural or historic interest – are subject to the provisions of an Act which makes it an offence to damage or alter them and also gives the local authority various powers to safeguard them. Buildings are graded in accordance with their architectural and/or historic importance. 'Listed building consent' is needed in order to demolish, alter or extend a listed building. They must be well maintained, and fines can be imposed for neglect or demolition.

Groups of buildings forming areas of special architectural or historic interest may be designated 'conservation areas' and special permission must be granted before any work is undertaken. Listed buildings and conservation areas are now quite common and many nursing homes, hostels, hotels and conference centres are housed in old mansions, mills or even warehouses which are 'listed'.

2 Building Regulations

These are concerned with the well-being of the public and not the building itself, as an insurance company may be. For instance, there is an insistence upon standards of construction which guard against the building's collapse and consequent injury to occupants and passers-by. Other concerns have become apparent recently which have extended this original view. The introduction to the regulations states:

'The main purpose of the Regulations is to ensure the health and safety of people in or about the building. They are *also* concerned with energy conservation and access to buildings for the disabled.'

When new building work is proposed, including alterations, annotated drawings have to be submitted to the building control officer to determine whether Regulations are being respected. Because there are many methods of construction and designers are ingenious, the Regulations cannot lay down hard and fast rulings. In the past, they have been couched in quasi-legal jargon and were open to interpretation. Indeed, books have been written to show architects what the typical results may be in constructional terms. The 1985 issue of Regulations initiated the idea of a series of working documents with illustrations, showing what is 'deemed to satisfy' Regulations. Materials, site preparation, thermal insulation, staircases and ramps, refuse disposal, sound insulation and structural fire precautions are amongst the topics covered. Regulations are constantly updated, and those concerning insulation and sanitary pipework, for example, were amended in 1990.

Architects must make sure that their design conforms to Regulations to ensure health and safety, and inspections are undertaken during construction, but of course there are always grey areas. Sometimes it is possible to achieve a 'relaxation' of regulations in one area if it can be shown that a building's other characteristics render it safe.

In Scotland, where there is a different legal system, the Building (Scotland) Acts apply, but the Building Standards Regulations are the same in spirit as the Building Regulations.

Planning consent and Building Regulations approval are of paramount importance and are an area in which professional help can be invaluable. Depending on the type of building, other legislation may also apply.

3 Fire Precautions Act 1971

Four categories of premises are covered by the Act, three of which are relevant here:

- places of amusement, recreation and public resort;
- residential establishments such as hotels, residential institutions and hospitals;
- educational establishments.

Certificates are issued by the local fire authority and premises must have a certificate in force. In particular, means of escape, means of fighting fires and means of warning (alarm) are the subjects of the fire officer's concern. In practice the implications are that escape routes are planned with fire doors, widths of corridors and openings, and positioning of extinguishers all taken into account. These are referred to in *British Standards Code of Practice* 3,

Chapter IV. Of course these regulations are of prime importance and they constitute constraints on the design of residential accommodation in particular. The manager must be aware of these regulations and inspect the premises regularly to ensure that they are maintained.

4 Other legislation

This affects different building types, including the Theatres Act 1968 and Cinematograph Act 1952; Offices, Shops & Railway Premises Act 1963; Food Hygiene (General) Regulations, 1970; Nursing Homes Act 1975; Defective Premises Act 1972; Health and Safety at Work etc Act 1974; and the Licensing Act 1964.

It falls outside the scope of this book to examine all the legislation applicable to the accommodation industry, but it should be noted that it is constantly changing, and managers should be aware of laws affecting the pursuit of their business.

5 Statutory undertaking

In the course of the building process it is inevitable that the various statutory undertakers will come into the picture at one stage or another. These are the sewer and highways authorities, and the gas, water and electricity supply undertakings.

In the case of drains from a building to a public sewer a right of connection exists, but written notice must be given to the local water authority which looks after drainage. In the case of water, gas and electricity supply, written notice of desire to connect to mains must be given. All of these undertakings are governed by their own Acts; for example, applications to the electricity authorities should state the maximum power required and its proposed use, in accordance with the Act.

In all of the cases where permission is required, it is perhaps best to enter into discussions informally with officers before making a formal application. In this way decisions may be reached by individuals giving positive responses rather than employing a system which vets and rejects in a negative spirit.

Facilities for the disabled

As has been seen, Building Regulations now take some notice of the problems of the disabled. Of course, it may be considered a moral duty on behalf of the building designer and owner to provide access for those who have physical disabilities, but in addition, it makes no sense commercially to restrict a whole section of potential clientele from access. Prior to the implementation of the 1985 Building Regulations, legislation concerned with providing access was persuasive rather than coercive. The Chronically Sick and Disabled Persons Act 1981 required that provision should be made in new public buildings in terms of access, parking and sanitary facilities for the disabled.

Approved Document M of the 1985 Building Regulations applies to offices, shops, educational establishments, principal entrance storeys of factories and public buildings. It reinforces the requirement for access for the physically disabled to be provided in new buildings and makes some provision for access to existing buildings. It is enforced at the discretion of building control officers. In other words, those anticipating constructing new buildings or extensions, or making alterations to existing buildings which fall into these categories, will probably have to make provision for access for the disabled if their proposals are to be approved.

There are British Standards which refer to access for the disabled and other government notes which are relevant such as Department of Education and Science *Design Note 18*, 1984 (*Educational Buildings*) and *Development Control Policy Note 16A*, 1986 (*Access for the Disabled*).

Exercises

1 Assess one area of a hospitality building in terms of:
   a) physical performance
   b) spatial provision
   c) appropriate characteristics.

2 Describe the character or style of a specific building and suggest how it might be used to promote the business which it houses.

3 Consider how existing hotel/hostel/club premises might be adapted to cope with a proposal to offer conference facilities. What factors must be considered? Outline your recommendations for either adapting the existing facilities, extending them or building a new block.

3 Construction and enclosure

Objectives

After reading this chapter you should:

- Be aware of the various types of structure used in building construction and where each is used to best advantage.
- Understand the methods of building construction used for foundations, floors, walls, openings, and roofs, and the materials from which they are made.
- Have an appreciation of the relationship between a building and its use of energy.
- Understand the importance and significance of maintaining the building structure.

This book does not set out to replace specialist texts on building construction which are already available. Instead, the aim in this chapter is to note some of the principles of construction and to explain how they influence the performance and potential of the building, so that the manager will have a better appreciation of both problems and opportunities when there is a need for change. In addition he or she will recognise the need for thoughtful maintenance procedures.

Where enclosure is to be provided, as described in Chapter 1, then enclosing elements have to be built in order to protect occupants. *Construction* is the technology that allows this to be achieved. *Structure* refers to the means by which elements such as roofs, floors, and walls are supported. A structural strategy is often decided early on in the design process, and as architects organise spaces and volumes they will think automatically of the structure that is necessary to support the building. This, in turn, interacts with other factors in the design process and influences the layout of the building and its final appearance. In many cases structure helps to give a broad underlying sense of visual organisation – a rhythm – to the building.

Structural systems

Commonly, two types of structural system are encountered in building design. *Loadbearing structures* are generally found in smaller scale buildings and in many of the buildings dating from before the turn of the century. The enclosing walls have a dual purpose – they protect, but they also support the roof and floors as well (*see* Fig 3.1). It is important, as far as possible, to retain the structural integrity of the loadbearing walls to prevent collapse. *Framed structures* provide support independent of enclosure. In other words, a system is employed whereby the loads are carried by one set of elements, and protection is afforded by another (*see* Fig 3.2).

Some buildings may be 'hybrids' or fall between the two types. Grand residential buildings in the nineteenth century, for example, may have been built with loadbearing walls of considerable thickness, but if large open spaces such as dining- or ballrooms were required, then frame elements – girders or joists – may have been introduced to span across openings. 'Cross wall' construction, on the other hand, has been used frequently in the twentieth century where buildings with multiple, repetitive cells were needed, for example, student hostels with rows of study bedrooms. Here the walls act as regular structural supports filled between with a light 'skin'.

The implications of structural types is of extreme importance when considering alterations. Removing parts of a loadbearing wall to create new windows or links through to an extension can prove problematic. It is very questionable in such structures to have more window than wall area, as the wall *is* the structure, and consequently there are limitations as to what can be achieved. Over-enthusiastic provision of openings can lead to structural failure. Similarly, it is important to understand the position of structural walls

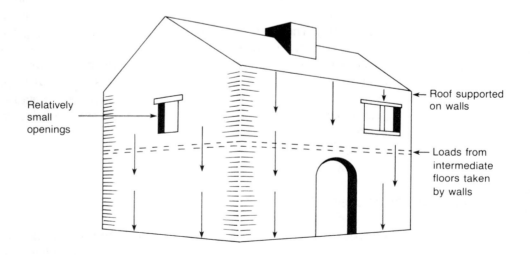

Relatively small openings

Roof supported on walls

Loads from intermediate floors taken by walls

Fig 3.1 Drawing showing the essentials of loadbearing construction

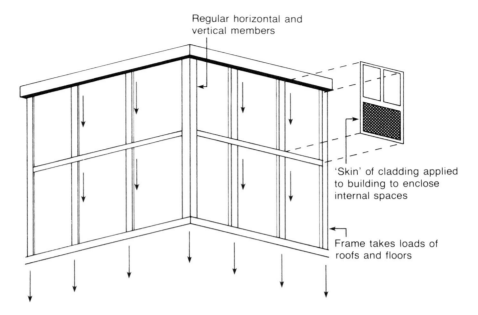

Regular horizontal and
vertical members

'Skin' of cladding applied
to building to enclose
internal spaces

Frame takes loads of
roofs and floors

Fig 3.2 Drawing showing the essentials of framed construction

when dealing with alterations inside a loadbearing building. There are
constraints upon what can be removed or how wide an opening may be.

In framed buildings, the external skin can be modified by removing
cladding panels and replacing them with windows or doors as necessary,
because the frame of the building is doing the structural work. In some
cases, however, the structure may be braced against the force of the wind by
some infill or cladding component, so it is best to seek specialist advice. In
general, though, framed structures are much more adaptable, both in terms
of the building's skin (or exterior) and internally, where walls can be non-
loadbearing. They can therefore be removed, replaced by glazed screens,
planting boxes, low walls or any other form of space-divider. Externally, a
fresh look could be given to the building by replacing a worn-out, thermally
inefficient skin by a new one. There are manufacturers who specialise in
systems of building cladding and a variety of types is available.

It is important now to consider some of the characteristics of both major
systems in more detail.

Loadbearing structures

Loadbearing structures operate according to the laws of gravity. It is this
force which enables the structure to work and, once defied, the
consequences may be spectacular. Traditionally, loadbearing construction
consists of small units of stone, brick or concrete blockwork bedded together

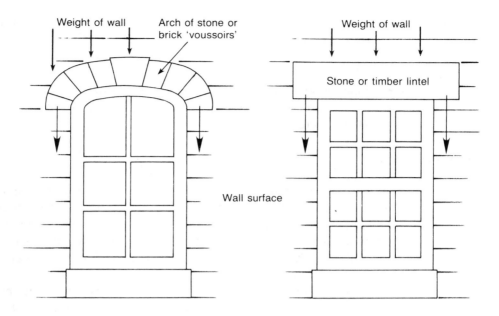

Fig 3.3 Openings in loadbearing walls

and relying on gravity to hold them in position. Mortar is not really an adhesive, merely a way of helping to stack the elements. Other materials may be used to produce a 'mass wall': for example, rammed earth which is used traditionally in some parts of the UK and other parts of the world. Openings in loadbearing structures are necessarily small. Traditionally they are represented by the arch and the lintel (*see* Fig 3.3).

The 'arch' uses the small units of the wall, forming an unbroken segment of a circle. Force from the wall above is transmitted around and down, and the blocks or 'voussoirs' squeeze together. The 'lintel' is a piece of stone or timber acting as a beam to span the opening and thus support the wall above. If the span is large these systems reach unmanageable proportions, which is why openings in loadbearing walls tend to be small in scale. Where strong, lightweight lintels fabricated from sheet steel are used, then spans can be much greater (e.g. the large picture window or patio door), but they can look quite odd when considered against the rest of the wall. Courses of brickwork can appear to 'float' over the opening.

Loadbearing construction is still common for smaller scale buildings, as it has been since the dawn of architecture. It is limited because of its rudimentary structural nature; it needs to be very thick at the bottom if the building is to be of any great height. At a small scale it is often associated with timber floors and roofs and the traditional domestic forms of house or inn.

Advantages

■ Elements both enclose and support.

- Small units give a human scale (brick size fits into the hand and thus relates to body size).

Disadvantages

- Loadbearing structures are not easily adapted.
- Walls and other elements grow to large proportions as the size of the building increases.

Framed structures

Framed structures are constructed normally out of high-strength materials such as steel or reinforced concrete. In loadbearing construction, planar elements, i.e. the walls, transmit loads. In framed construction linear elements, the columns and beams of the frame, transmit loads. In conventional modern construction, frames consist of components that are, in essence, no more structurally advanced than Stonehenge.

Usually, a grid of columns (vertical elements) is worked out by the architect concurrent with the general design and planning, so that a sensible regular arrangement of columns is produced, responding to the plan form. A regular grid is convenient because it means, roughly speaking, that all the loads imposed on the building (including the weight of the structure itself, the weight of occupants, furniture and equipment and the loads imposed by wind and snow) are evenly split up. Therefore, the sizes of the columns and beams can be consistent. This makes construction easier, and allows for standardisation of elements, such as infill panels and window frames. If the use of the building necessitates several floors of similar accommodation, then the repetitious regular grid form is ideal (*see* Fig 3.4).

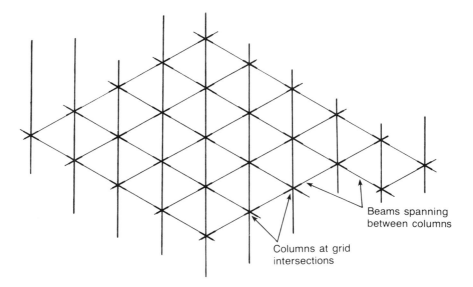

Beams spanning
between columns

Columns at grid
intersections

Fig 3.4 The regular grid of a framed structure

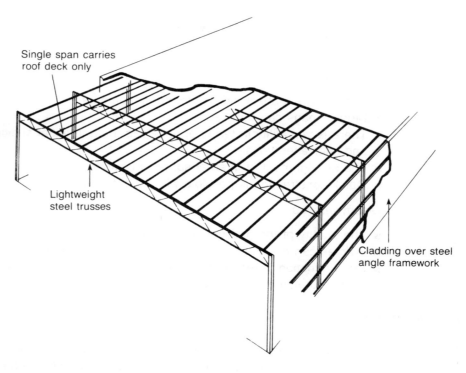

Single span carries
roof deck only

Lightweight
steel trusses

Cladding over steel
angle framework

Fig 3.5 A long span, single storey structure

Not all frames form this sort of regular 'cage'. *Portal frames* are commonly used for large single-storey buildings such as factories and warehouses, but also for low-cost sports facilities and community buildings. They are spaced regularly, but provide a 'clear' span. They are often made of steel or laminated timber members. Long span structures invariably use frameworks, perhaps with columns grouped at either side of the space with large built-up trusses running between, in order to support a roof in one clear span over an uninterrupted volume (*see* Fig 3.5). Roofs and walls may have their own particular frames. For instance in timber 'balloon frame' buildings, popular in rural districts of North America, the walls themselves are framed from timber and carry floor and roof structures.

As has been seen, unlike loadbearing construction, the elements in framed structures split up their responsibilities between loadcarrying and enclosure, so that the frame has to have an 'overcoat'. The overcoat's job depends on where the building is. In Northern Europe it has to keep weather out, keep heat in, provide protection from sun, give privacy and so on. Internal partitions have no weather-proofing tasks, but their functions can vary. They may need to offer acoustic privacy, visual screening or space division. Whole ranges of materials can be used, from the Japanese timber-framed houses with paper walls, through to stone-clad, prestige city centre hotels. Designers are given the freedom to create their own cladding or use one of a number of proprietory systems available from manufacturers, which vary from the type found in cheap warehouses to very expensive systems for high quality accommodation.

Advantages

- Less space is absorbed by structural elements.
- Bigger spans can be used.
- There is versatility in terms of envelope, both in initial choice of materials and later alterations.
- The arrangement of internal space is flexible.
- Quick construction is possible with steel frames.

Disadvantages

- The rigidity of the grid may cramp design.
- Frames can be expensive, depending how and when used.
- Fire protection is required, e.g. a steel frame needs concrete casing or a coating of flame-resistant paint in most circumstances.

Other types of structure

Over recent years, more advanced structural types have been developed in order to maximise spans and minimise the amount of structural material required.

1 Mast and bracing-type structure
   The mast and bracing-type structure exploits the tensile strength of materials, such as the resistance of steel to stretching. It is a distinctive and structurally efficient way of covering large, clear-span spaces without intermediate supports. Tall steel masts support cables that hold up roof structures. There are problems in terms of external maintenance, however, and in protecting the structure from chemical attack and corrosion. Structures such as these are used for prestigious large-scale show rooms, sports halls and swimming pools.

2 Space frames
   The structures discussed so far tend to be made as a series of separate items which are bolted together. However, space frames are designed as a three-dimensional whole and are therefore very rigid. The construction of racing cars and some types of aircraft provides a useful analogy.
   'Space decks' are three-dimensional roof structures which are composed, typically, of prefabricated tubular steel or aluminium 'pyramids' bolted together to form fairly deep but very strong roofs. Large clean spans are possible with a minimal number of supports.

3 Inflatable structures
   These can be composed of a series of inflated ribs with light fabric infill, or

Fig 3.6   A tent-like structure: The Schlumberger Building

they may be bubble-like, the whole skin being supported by increased internal air pressure provided by blowers. This is a very efficient way of covering a large area with a lightweight skin. Unfortunately, any access is limited, because of the need to provide an airlock to prevent deflation. They are often used for storage or where a large area needs to be covered relatively cheaply without intermediate support, e.g. an exhibition building.

4 Tents

As the name suggests, these structures are based on a commonplace idea, yet very beautiful results are possible when translated to a large scale. Huge steel masts are used and either a grid of cables or a tough constructional textile is pulled over and between the masts. The stretched fabric and, usually, additional tension wires are held down to the ground at strong anchorage points (*see* Fig 3.6). If used over a large area, this is an efficient means of enclosing space, but small-scale versions can be more expensive than conventional structures.

5 Concrete shells

Reinforced concrete need not be a 'lumpy' or dense material, but can be used to form a thin shell to enclose space. These shells rely on the use of three-dimensional geometric forms, such as the hyperbolic paraboloid (a two-way curve), to generate a rigid yet delicate structure (*see* Fig 3.7). They were popular particularly in the 1960s, but are expensive to build and maintain; also, unusable internal space is often the by-product of a spectacular external appearance.

It is impossible to describe all of these structural types in detail here. Most are used for non-residential accommodation, and are subject to variations where used. It is very likely, however, that they will continue to increase in popularity for buildings such as leisure pools, sports centres and entertainment complexes.

Fig 3.7 Reinforced concrete 'shells': Sydney Opera House (Photograph courtesy of the Government of New South Wales, Australia)

Elements of construction

The accommodation manager should not have to cope unaided with major structural problems, but must have an appreciation of how the structure is to be maintained. This applies not only to rigidity, but, for example, to the preservation of any fireproof coatings and to the prevention of corrosion and long-term deterioration of materials.

Foundations

Foundations form an 'intermediary' in the transmission of loads from the building to the ground. Loads reach the foundations either via the structural frame of the building, or through load-bearing walls. Such loads are imposed by the self-weight of the structure and by the contents of the building: people, furniture, equipment and machinery. The weather also plays its part, and a heavy snowfall can add considerably to the overall weight on the roof structure. Wind loads are normally horizontal, and are usually resolved within the building fabric by use of bracing.

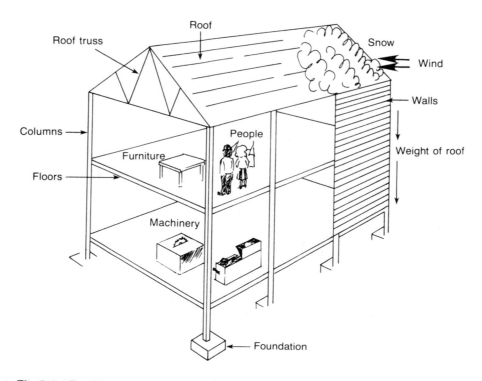

Fig 3.8 Drawing showing the elements of construction

It is vital for the engineer or architect to know the bearing capacity of the ground, i.e. how heavy a load it will take, and what pressure is to be placed upon it by the foundations. If the ground is incapable of supporting the load, the building will collapse. The type of foundation used, therefore, will vary with these conditions. The accommodation manager must appreciate that any planned extensions must take account of this.

Strip foundations

These are commonly used in loadbearing structures where continuous support is needed. Mass concrete is generally considered the most suitable material for the purpose. Concrete is made by mixing cement, sand and other stone aggregates together with water. The chemical reaction that occurs binds all elements together to produce what is, essentially, an artificial stone. The ratios of the mixture and the type of aggregate used can be varied depending on the intended purpose of the concrete. Mass concrete for strip footings is usually of comparatively low strength and as its appearance is not important expensive aggregates can be avoided.

The width of the foundation depends upon the area required to spread the load (*see* Fig 3.9). Strip foundations may be laid at the bottom of a trench and brickwork built up, or, as is increasingly common, the whole trench filled with concrete if the foundation needs to be no wider than the excavator

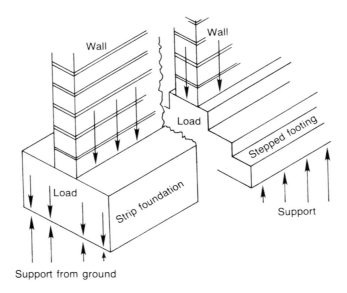

Fig 3.9 Strip foundations

bucket. In the case of older buildings, foundations may be found where the brick or stonework spreads to transmit the load. These are known as 'stepped footings'.

Pad foundations

Pads are used under columns in framed structures. As it is only the column that transmits the load, so only the area beneath it needs a foundation. Concrete foundation pads are calculated to spread the load depending upon soil-bearing capacity. They are usually reinforced with steel bars to prevent snapping.

Rafts

Sometimes buildings are constructed on huge reinforced concrete rafts to spread the load across soil of poor bearing capacity.

Piles

These are of several types, but are normally employed where the building needs to be supported on deep strata. Traditional piling in historic buildings consists of timber posts hammered down through the soil. In modern buildings reinforced concrete piles are used which may be hammered, bored or vibrated into position. Piles can be regarded as columns supporting the building.

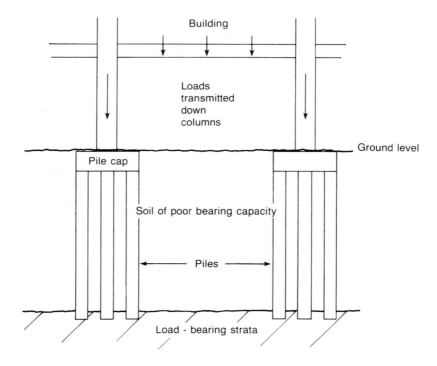

Fig 3.10   Piled foundations

Floors

Solid

Unless the building has a basement, the purpose of the ground floor is to protect the inhabitants from bare earth, moisture and plant growth. Simple, solid ground floors consist of a slab of heavy, dense material, usually concrete, with a membrane to prevent moisture penetration and a surface 'finish', all resting on well-consolidated hardcore (*see* Fig 3.11). Thick floors of this type will invariably be used where heavy equipment is to be found, such as laundry machinery.

Suspended

Traditional, too, are suspended timber ground floors where lighter loads are encountered. 'Sleeper walls' are built up and timber joists laid on top of them (*see* Fig 3.12). A board or sheet finish is applied to aid rigidity as well as provide a surface for other finishes. Floors such as these should be well-ventilated to prevent rot in the timber. Air circulation is effected by means of air bricks in external walls, which should never be covered, and gaps in the brickwork of the sleeper walls. 'Strutting' is used between joists to make the floor rigid and to prevent joist movement.

Upper floors are, of course, 'suspended'. In other words, they are

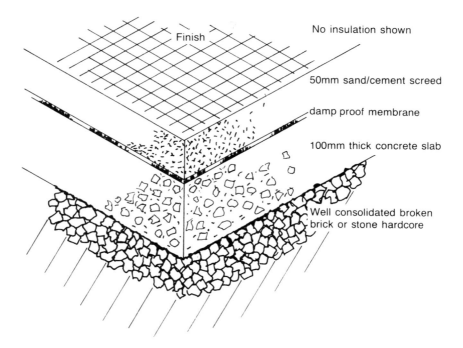

Finish

No insulation shown

50mm sand/cement screed

damp proof membrane

100mm thick concrete slab

Well consolidated broken brick or stone hardcore

Fig 3.11 A solid ground floor

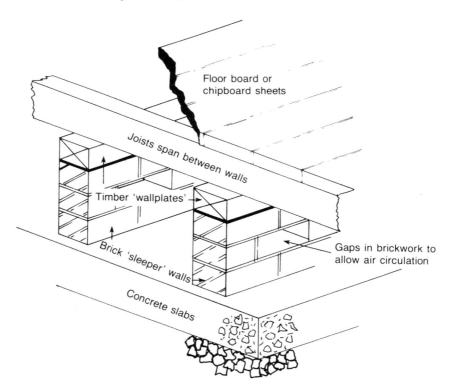

Floor board or chipboard sheets

Joists span between walls

Timber 'wallplates'

Brick 'sleeper' walls

Gaps in brickwork to allow air circulation

Concrete slabs

Fig 3.12 A suspended timber ground floor

supported either by walls or by beams and columns. Small-scale work, traditionally, uses appropriately sized softwood joists, their depth depending on span. The joists support timber boarding or chipboard panelling. Where openings have to be made in a floor, for instance where a staircase breaks through, then large sized joists are employed to 'trim' the others and to provide support around the hole. Timber strutting is used in between the joists to provide rigidity. Traditionally, carpentry jointing techniques were used, but nowadays proprietory products are employed such as pressed metal timber connectors and joist hangers, as illustrated in Fig 3.13. In bigger, framed buildings where either steel or concrete is used, a timber floor can be employed subject to the constraints of loading and other factors such as fire resistance. Timber is severely limited in terms of span, however.

If an '*in situ*' concrete frame has been used then it is probable that the '*in situ*' concrete floor will be in evidence. '*In situ*' means that the concrete is mixed on site or arrives 'already mixed' and is placed in moulds of formwork and left to cure and become solid. The building grows outwards and upwards as the casting process progresses. The floor 'slabs' are part of this process. There are several variations upon the basic theme.

Some buildings are made from 'pre-cast' concrete, where the various elements are produced in a factory and transported to site for assembly. If a large, steel-framed building is being built, pre-cast reinforced concrete planks, which span between the steel beams of the structural 'cage', can be used.

Nearly all concrete used for anything but simple strip footings and infill work is 'reinforced'. This is because although the material is strong in compression and can withstand high loads before cracking or crumbling, it is relatively weak in tension. A concrete beam would easily crack if loaded. Steel bars are therefore introduced and sometimes a steel mesh is used.

There are many types of composite construction in evidence where

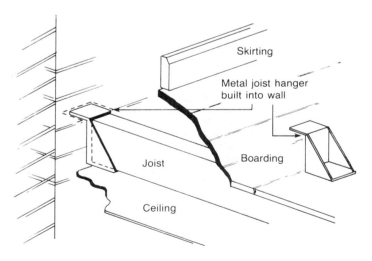

Fig 3.13 A 'joist hanger', used for a suspended upper floor

combinations of steel and concrete are to be found, particularly in older buildings. Indeed, in Victorian times, concrete was used in conjunction with iron beams to provide 'fireproof' floors. Today, 'compartmentalisation' of the building into various zones with certain degrees of fire resistance is an important factor in design. The fire resistance of floors must be considered so that a blaze will not spread from one part of a building to another inside a set time (*see* Chapter 8).

External walls

Some of the more advanced, modern types of structure do not have walls as such, that is, the delineation between what is 'roof' and what is 'wall' is not clear. In traditional structures, however, the distinction is perfectly clear. The walls are the vertical, protecting, and enclosing elements (*see* Chapter 1) and the roof sits on top with its own separate structure.

In the past, traditional loadbearing walls would be made thick enough to transmit loads from the roof and intermediate floor to the foundations without failing in compression, buckling or overturning. It was, however, possible for walls to allow dampness to soak through. The 'cavity' wall (illustrated in Fig 3.14) was developed to prevent this from happening.

The 'outer leaf' of a cavity wall can be made of a high quality, relatively expensive finish, such as a 'facing' brick to give an attractive external appearance. Any rain soaking through this is prevented from being transmitted to the interior by the cavity. The 'inner leaf' can fulfill two basic functions:

■ it carries compressive forces from the roof and intermediate floors to the foundation

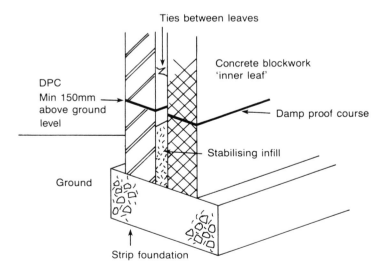

Fig 3.14 Base of a cavity wall

■ it provides thermal insulation which prevents heat from being lost from within the building.

Further insulation can be added in the cavity or attached to the outside wall. (Thermal insulation, an important consideration, is dealt with as a separate topic towards the end of this chapter.) Outer and inner leaves are tied together by plastic or steel cavity ties which allow some sharing of the structural function.

The wall above ground level is prevented from becoming damp through rising ground moisture by the insertion of a *damp-proof course* consisting of a strip of suitable impermeable material, such as bitumen felt or plastic, inserted between courses (lines of brickwork). Modern buildings are constructed with damp-proof courses, but many old buildings are perpetually damp and need a damp-proof course insertion. This can be done by electrolytic means, where a moisture-repelling resin is introduced into the wall, or by sawing into a horizontal joint and sliding in the waterproof material.

Essentially, then, loadbearing construction must be stable and weatherproof. Trouble starts when anything happens to the fabric to cause these conditions not to be fulfilled. For instance, the damp-proof course may be broken or moisture may find a route around it; the cavity may be bridged and driving rain may soak the wall, transmitting moisture to the inner leaf.

Openings

Particular care has to be taken around openings for doors and windows, both from the point of view of structure and damp penetration. Figure 3.15

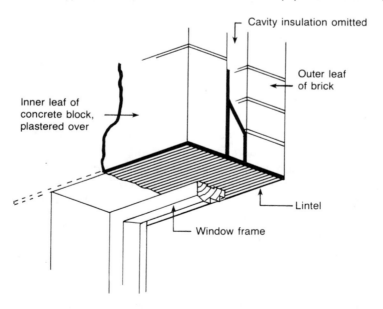

Fig 3.15 The head of an opening supported by a pressed steel lintel

represents modern practice in traditional small-scale loadbearing structures. The pressed steel lintels illustrated are a fairly recent innovation. In the past, problems occurred at openings in attempting to support both leaves of the wall without water penetration, or in the creation of 'cold bridges' across the structure. Although it is normally necessary to have openings in walls these are best minimised in loadbearing construction. They are potential trouble spots, and the more junctions, discontinuities, changes of material and plane, the more likely trouble is. It is worth noting, from a maintenance point of view, that extra attention should be paid to these areas.

Where a wall has to be punctured many times to provide a large amount of natural light, it may be better designed as a framed, rather than loadbearing, structure.

Windows

Windows can have fixed lights — glass held directly in the frame — or they can have casements, which consist of a main frame fitted into the building structure and a glazed sash (the sash is the part of the window which opens). There are many possible variations depending on materials used, the configuration of opening and fixed lights, and the type of sash. Wide ranges are available from manufacturers ready made, or windows can be purpose-made according to the design of the building.

Timber is the traditional material for window frames, both softwood and hardwood. Joinery manufacturers usually make frames in sizes to fit standard openings based on brick dimensions. Because wood is easily worked, special windows can be designed and made without trouble. It is essential that softwood is covered with a protective coating to prevent rot and that generous sills (usually called cills by architects) are provided to throw water clear of the frame (Fig 3.16). Because of the need for regular repainting and maintenance, *UPVC* (plastic) window frames have found favour in places where timber windows would normally be used. They are self-coloured, can be washed clean and require little attention, but the range of sections from which windows are made up is limited. The delicate appearance of some timber frames cannot be achieved.

Steel frames became fashionable during the 1920s and 1930s and were very popular in the years immediately after the Second World War. Like timber, they need regular attention to prevent deterioration. In addition to normal oxidation (causing rust), exposure to salt air in seaside areas adds to corrosion. They also have poor insulative properties and in warm rooms condensation easily forms on the frame members. *Aluminium* window frames are now more widely used and hollow sections can be filled with insulative material. The aluminium can be powder coated to give an attractive, coloured, hard-wearing finish, requiring little maintenance, or it may be protectively anodised.

Most types of window frame can be designed either to accept sealed double glazing units or to make provision for a glazed inner frame.

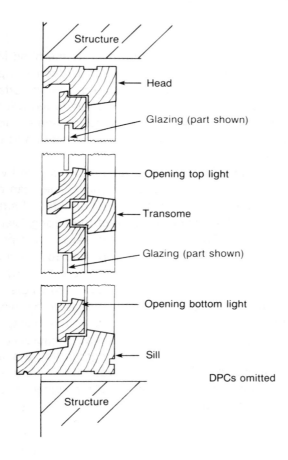

Fig 3.16 Section through a timber casement

Casements may have hinged, pivoted or sliding sashes. The use of hinges is limited in terms of the size of sash to be supported. A heavy sash could pull the hinge away from the frame, and a larger hinge is impracticable because of frame size. Aluminium windows are strong and relatively light and so larger opening lights are possible. These are usually pivoted and have friction stays which prevent them from swinging out uncontrollably. Such casements can be made reversible, so that in tall buildings windows can be cleaned from the inside.

Sliding sashes were commonplace in the nineteenth century, but fell out of favour because of the extensive maintenance required to keep them in good order. In fact, the vertically sliding sash is a very useful building element. Either the bottom, the top or both 'leaves' of the window can be opened and finely adjusted to achieve ventilation without the kind of draughts and disruption associated with a hung sash. Better materials, mechanisms and wood treatments may help them to return to popularity, though they are more expensive than standard types.

Doors

Like windows, doors generally consist of a main frame fitted into the structural opening, with whatever kind of shutter is deemed appropriate hung from the frame. Doors and building entrances have an important symbolic significance and care and thought should be given to individual designs. In practical terms, however, the door should be sturdy and durable, should open in the manner appropriate to the kind of traffic expected and secure the premises when closed.

Timber doors are traditional in small-scale premises, fitted within a softwood frame, with a sturdy hardwood threshold. They can be made by framing and panelling, or be 'double-skin', with an internal structure. *Glazed* doors often have a metal structure because of the strong, slender members needed to hold the glass. Specialised doors for large-scale premises may be required to permit the access of vehicles. Top-hung roller shutters, sliding and folding and metal panelled vertical sliding doors of many types are available. Side-hung *rubber* doors are frequently used where there is constant traffic and the leaves of the door can be pushed aside by vehicles or trolleys. They fall back into position to prevent draughts or the leakage of warm air.

Description of every type of door manufactured is impractical, but given a well-defined need or set of criteria it is fairly certain that a suitable type can be found. Means of operating the door are varied, too, from the simple spring-loaded door closer, through to electrically powered mechanisms activated by pressure pads or photo-electric cells.

Materials

The traditional materials used in loadbearing construction have already been noted: brick, stone and concrete block. There is no reason why other materials with similar properties could not be used instead. Brick, however, remains a firm favourite.

Brick

Bricks are burnt clay blocks, the appearance of the brick being governed by the local clay. Since the Industrial Revolution some types of brick have become particularly popular because they are relatively cheap and easily mass-produced.

Bricks are designed to be handled. This is the basis of their size and proportion, and they can be easily built into a wall by 'bonding'. Their properties are well known: hard, durable and strong in compression, but not commendable from an insulative point of view. A major advantage is the number of different types available. *Common bricks* are for general constructional duties, *engineering bricks* for heavy structural work and *facing bricks* for areas exposed to view. These may be multiplied by the fact that manufacturers produce ranges of bricks of varying shapes, colours and textures. Bricks are usually 215mm x 102.5mm x 65mm, but co-ordinating dimensions of bricks plus a mortar joint are 225mm x 112.5mm x 75mm.

Bricks are assembled into a wall by building up layers. Vertical joints between bricks are filled with cement/sand mortar and horizontal beds between layers are spread with mortar in order to seat the next course. Although in practice some adhesive properties may be present, mortar is not recognised as 'sticking the bricks' from a structural point of view. Wall building is organised so that vertical joints in successive layers do not coincide. This is known as *bonding* and there are various types which can be noted by observation, but which do not need explanation here. 'Specials' (special bricks to customer's or designer's requirements) can be produced for window sills and plinths.

Stone

Stone is an indigenous material in upland areas, for example in the Cotswolds and Pennines. It was used traditionally where quarrying was 'local' to site. With the spread of mass-produced bricks during the nineteenth century it became less popular. It was, however, exported to all parts of the country for use in high-quality buildings. The extent and character of its use depends upon the qualities of the stone. If easily worked, as is the case with some limestones, the character of buildings will be different to that in areas where the stone is hard or coarse and difficult to carve.

There are too many variations to describe here, but in principle the way in which stone walls are built depends upon local tradition, which in turn is based upon the nature of the stone and its ease of use. The local planning officer may well have leaflets showing examples of typical practice for potential builders to examine and follow. Generally, though, stone is sawn into useable and fairly uniform chunks for building purposes. High-quality, very finely sawn stone is known as 'ashlar' masonry.

Concrete blockwork

Concrete blockwork seems, at first, rather unappealing. There are, however, several different types and it is a very useful material. Dense blocks are strong and can be used for loadbearing walls or in situations that may be damp. Lightweight blocks, of which there are several proprietary brands, have good thermal insulation properties and it is possible to build an inner leaf from blockwork which is strong enough to support conventional domestic scale construction and have reasonable insulative values. *Fair faced blocks*, i.e. blocks with an attractive surface, are obtainable which can be left exposed or painted.

Blocks are available in various thicknesses and are much larger than bricks (450mm x 102mm) which makes for rapid construction. *Reconstituted stone blocks* can be obtained which are made from ground-up stone and cement; these give the colour of stone but are in fact regular, easy to build, man-made artefacts. Advances have been made in appearance in recent years and good quality reconstituted stone/cement blocks can sometimes pass for the real thing.

Walls in framed construction may appear to be quite insubstantial because of their reduced duties. This does not mean that materials usually associated with loadbearing construction cannot be used. Indeed, stone- and brick-clad framed buildings are particularly common in cities where architects have wished to provide civic buildings with traditional signs of wealth, prestige and stability. Here, the loadbearing structure merely supports itself and is tied back to the steel frame or fills in as panels between the frame's members.

There is an opportunity with framed construction, though, to keep down the self-weight of the building and to open up the façade so that it can be glazed or partially glazed, giving light, bright spaces. The enthusiasm for this among architects of the 1950s and 1960s unfortunately led to large buildings with totally glazed façades which usually did little to prevent exposure to the blazing sun in summer, or terrific heat-loss in winter. Lightweight walls do not necessarily mean glazing, however. Manufacturers produce panel systems with standard support grids which can be adapted to new buildings. These panels may be made of pressed steel or aluminium and are often formed into a sandwich, with a smooth, coloured, plastic-coated outer skin, plastic foam insulation interior, and self-finished internal surface (*see* Fig 3.17). GRP (glass reinforced plastic) is also a popular material for such panels. These panels are fixed back to the supporting grid, which itself is bolted to the building frame, and sealed between with neoprene (synthetic rubber) gaskets which prevent rain penetration. Unlike traditional loadbearing materials, the panels of plastic-coated steel and GRP are available in bright colours.

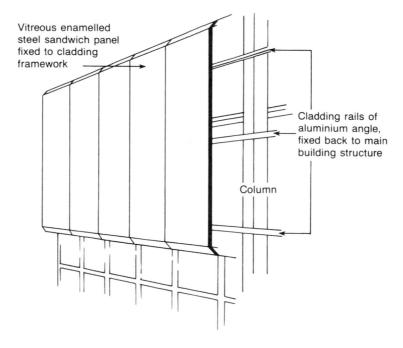

Vitreous enamelled
steel sandwich panel
fixed to cladding
framework

Cladding rails of
aluminium angle,
fixed back to main
building structure

Column

Fig 3.17 Cladding system for a framed building

Precast concrete

Precast, factory made, concrete units can be bolted to a subframework and used as an effective cladding.Various interesting aggregates can be included to enhance the building's appearance and character. These panels are heavy, but can be made very accurately.

Glazing

'Patent glazing' and 'curtain walling' systems with subframes and grids are usually used if the façade is to be fully glazed. It should be noted, though, that self-supporting, large-scale glazing is now available. Large sheets of extremely strong glass are fastened back to the building structure to prevent movement caused by wind pressure and are fixed to each other by corner plates. The gaps between the glass are then filled by a polysulphide sealant.

In the case of a new building care should be taken to see that unpleasant conditions are not created by a large amount of glazing. The orientation should be checked so that solar heat gain is not excessive. Heat loss should be calculated. If a building is already largely glazed and suffers environmentally as a result, then thought must be given to internal and external screens, blinds and sun-breaks and to means of insulation, such as double or triple glazing. The glazed panels or the whole façade could be replaced by solid, insulated panels.

Internal walls

In loadbearing structures some of the internal walls will be active in supporting the structure. However, some walls may be partitions only. In framed structures internal walls are invariably partitions or screens with no structural work to do except in the case of, say, liftshafts or stairwells where structural walls run up through the building. How partitions or screens are made depends upon the work they have to do; an 'open' area with some need for delineation of separate spaces may have glazed screens with timber or aluminium frames. These can be purchased from manufacturers who specialise in partitioning. Similar systems with opaque panels can be obtained where visual privacy is required. Non-loadbearing 'studding' partitions are common. The builder simply erects a frame of, for example, 4" x 2" (100mm x 50mm) softwood 'studs' and 'noggins' and covers both sides with sheets of plasterboard. If acoustic privacy is required then heavy partitions may have to be made using concrete blockwork or brick. Planters and low walls can also be used to delineate spaces.

Roofs

Roofs are very potent symbols of shelter and security, especially pitched roofs. The roof's primary duty, however, is to keep out rain and to provide shelter from the sun. In the damp climates of north-west Europe too many flat roofs have failed to fulfil this function.

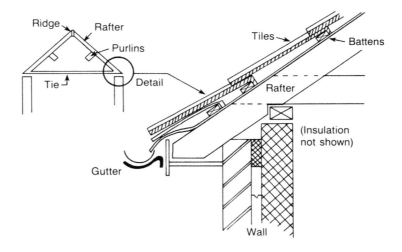

Fig 3.18 Section through the eaves of a pitched roof

Pitched roofs

Enormous pitched roof structures were at one time derided as being a waste of materials and space. It is only too obvious, though, that such roofs are traditional in the wetter parts of the world for very good practical reasons. Unfortunately, when a building reaches a large size or is complex, the incorporation of pitched roofs in design becomes difficult.

Pitched roofs are traditional in the British Isles. They are usually made up of timber rafters set at an angle, and covered by small units which overlap to prevent rain from entering, as shown in Fig 3.18. These units are generally slates (thin sheets of metamorphic rock dug from quarries) or tiles of clay or concrete. The result is a heavy covering which limits spans in timber roofs. These can be improved by using *trusses* and *purlins*. Purlins are beams running between cross walls which help to support rafters at some point along their length. Trusses are structural members which are far stronger than conventional rafters and ties, and can be used to support purlins. In some modern lightweight roofs 'trussed rafters' made from small section softwood are used in place of conventional rafters. Steel trusses enable greater distances to be spanned.

In pitched roofs, however, a problem occurs in that the greater the span, the higher the roof. The pitch could be reduced to counteract this, but unit materials such as slate do not perform adequately below a certain pitch. In some plan forms it is possible to use multiple pitched roofs, as illustrated in Fig 3.19. Unfortunately, roofs of this type possess internal gutters within the depth of the plan. Should the gutter finish fail or become congested with leaves or other debris, then water will leak down into the rooms below. Maintenance is a tricky problem.

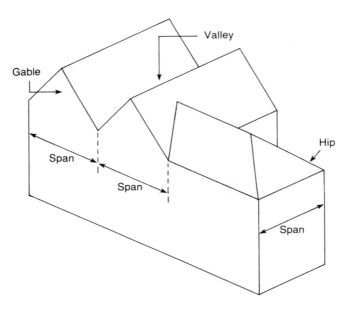

Fig 3.19 Multiple pitched roof arrangement

Flat roofs

Flat roofs are the logical outcome of the framed, grid building. There are proprietary roofing systems, but in elementary terms the typical flat roof consists of:

- support (beams/joists)
- insulation
- decking (concrete planks, metal decking, plywood)
- waterproof surface.

There is a great deal of freedom in planning below flat roofs compared to pitched roofs. Long spans can also be achieved quite easily. Problems occur, however, with the covering materials. 'Flat' roofs are usually 'laid to a fall' so that rainwater drains off in a predictable direction, but should the material be breached then water will flood into the building. Unfortunately, this often occurs as roofing materials are subject to considerable expansion and contraction (e.g. arising from exposure to the sun) which leads to fracturing. In addition, some materials may become brittle. Jointing is a problem where sheets of material meet, and failure can occur here, too. If there is access to the roof, then the covering can be damaged by impact loads, including those imposed by boot heels.

Good quality flat roof materials are expensive, for example, sheet metals such as copper and lead. Asphalt may be used, generally on top of a reinforced concrete roof deck, but this is subject to expansion and

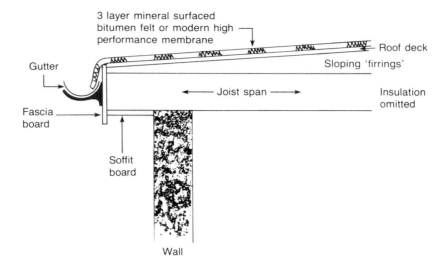

Fig 3.20 Section through the edge of a flat roof (simplified)

contraction problems. Bitumen felt is common and relatively cheap, but needs replacing after a few years, though surfacing with mineral chippings helps to reflect heat which would otherwise be absorbed (*see* Fig 3.20).

Advantages of pitched roofs

- Symbolically appropriate or 'satisfying'
- Internal space can be utilised for accommodation and storage if the structure is appropriate
- Long lasting and hard wearing with comparatively little maintenance.

Disadvantages of pitched roofs

- Spans limited
- Geometry of roof limits planning
- Lack of plan flexibility
- If the structure is heavy, the roof space will be limited so that there is a lot of structure for no extra space.

Advantages of flat roofs

- As long as the means of support can be clearly organised, it is relatively easy to roof any plan form and span.
- No excessive structure or volume
- Space on top can be used

Disadvantages of flat roofs

- Leaks easily develop
- Careful maintenance is required
- Building is abruptly terminated visually.

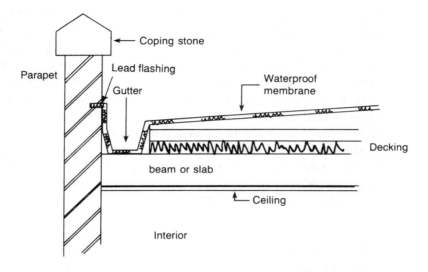

Fig 3.21 A gutter concealed behind a parapet (simplified)

Rainwater removal

If it is assumed that the plot on which the building stands is virgin site, then rain falling upon the field will soak into the soil and drain away naturally. Replacing this area with a roofed building means that, providing the roof is working properly, all rain will have to be disposed of via a drainage system. *Gutters* catch the rain from sloping surfaces and transmit it to *downpipes* which take it to *below ground drainage* (*see* Chapter 4). Gutters and rainwater pipes, today, are usually made of plastic and fixed to the eaves of building. Some gutters, though, may be part of the building structure, as is the case in a roof with a parapet (*see* Fig 3.21). Gutters may be obvious trouble-spots if not regularly cleaned and maintained and continuity of waterproof material checked. All gutters and downpipes must remove water directly so that it does not damage either the building's contents or fabric itself, which will deteriorate if constantly soaked.

Energy, insulation and enclosure

Heat

One of the chief functions of the building fabric is to help conserve energy. Fuel is burnt inside a building in order to keep the occupants warm. If the heat is allowed to escape rapidly, and more fuel needs to be burned to replace it, then this is a waste not only of money, but of precious fuel reserves. Indeed, it was the prompting of escalating energy prices due to the oil crisis of the early 1970s that focused attention on the energy conservation issue. Since then, Building Regulations have incorporated a section on the desirable minimum in terms of the *thermal performance* of the building fabric (Part 'L', 'Conservation of fuel and power'). The term *'U' value* is often used in this connection. It signifies the quantity of heat which flows from hot to cold through the building's skin, in other words, *thermal transmittance*. The higher the 'U' value, the more heat is lost. Although given as a value without units, it is measured as watts/square metre/degree centigrade. Thus, a single-glazed window has a 'U' value of 5.1, whereas modern domestic wall construction would aim to achieve a minimum overall 'U' value of about 0.45. Traditional heavyweight materials do not usually have very good 'U' values, but lightweight materials, where air is trapped in their structures, are much better insulators. Plastic foam of various kinds, and aereated concrete blocks, for example, are good insulators.

Walls

It is fairly certain that the walls of older buildings will not have good insulative properties, and measures to remedy this can be taken by adding suitable materials. It should be noted, though, that trouble may occur if simplistic solutions are sought and it is best to consult an independent specialist before attempting to upgrade the fabric. Particularly significant is the fact that poorly sited insulation may lead to warm air condensing out *within* the fabric, giving rise to long-term damage. There are problems, too, with foam insulants in cavity walls, where moisture can find its way through hairline cracks in the foam from the outer to the inner leaf.

Warmth does not simply escape through the walls, though, and some other considerations are important.

Roofs

Warm air rises, and may continue to do so up to the roof space. Heat then escapes through the thin fabric of the roof covering unless insulating material, such as a fibreglass quilt, is placed within the space. Care should be taken to insulate any pipework or storage tanks within the space.

Floors

Suspended ground floors may require insulation for the same reason as the roof fabric, i.e. the lightness of the structure and/or its lack of insulative value.

Openings

Windows are a weak zone in the envelope. One sheet of thin window glass has a very high 'U' value. Two sheets are a slight improvement, but results are vastly improved if an air space is located between the sheets, as air is a very good insulator. Double glazing is thus formed. The air gap has to be quite narrow to prevent the formation of convection currents.

Ill-fitting components

These can lead to heat escaping and cold air entering a building. Door and window frames are particular trouble spots, although it is often possible to deal with these simply by the use of sealing compounds and draught strips.

Ventilation

In order to ensure the well-being of occupants by supplying adequate oxygen, stale air has to be removed and fresh air drawn in from outside the building. If the stale air has been heated, as is likely in winter, then the energy used will be lost if it is simply expelled as exhaust. Heat recovery systems can be used to ensure that such waste is minimised (*see* Chapter 5).

Insulative materials, of course, can also be used where heat flow is *into* the building. In northern Europe this is usually due to the direct action of the sun, and can be dealt with most effectively by reflecting the rays away or by use of glazing that cuts out part of the spectrum of sunlight. The building's orientation and the position of any glazing relative to the sun should have been noted and allowed for during design.

Energy strategy and enclosure

Energy strategy and energy issues, such as solar energy, are fully discussed in Chapter 5. However, the role played by the skin of the building is important in conserving energy and reducing energy costs. Control of the energy used inside the building by insulation, altering patterns of use, heat recovery and use of renewable energy sources may all form part of an energy strategy.

The rays of the sun, absorbed by a thick, dark-painted wall, will later radiate into the building in the cool of the evening. Heat collected during the summer can be stored underground for release during winter.

These are sophisticated aspects of energy strategy. At a more fundamental level, the question of how the building is to behave must be considered. A lightweight, well-insulated structure, used frequently, may be left to cool down after use, but rapidly filled with warm air by powerful blowers just prior to operation. A heavyweight building with thick walls may be constantly topped up with small quantities of heat in the knowledge that once the heavy structure becomes warm it constantly contributes to a warm environment and the initial heating cost is not lost. Some sort of strategy should therefore be devised depending upon the nature of the envelope.

Sound

One further aspect of the building enclosure's function as a filter or insulator is that of noise. Much has been researched and written on this topic, and ideally, of course, a building should not be situated in an area where external noise levels are at variance with the building's purpose. However, in an imperfect world, the effects of any loud external sound can be rectified by screening the building with trees, mounds and fences. The last line of defence, however, is the building enclosure itself. Unlike heat insulation, sound insulation depends upon mass. The heavier a material is, generally speaking, the better it is at sound insulation. Unfortunately, weak spots may occur: roofs are usually lightweight, and window glazing transmits noises easily; any holes or gaps in the structure of any size render even the heaviest materials useless. Impact sounds, such as rain on the roof or hammering, are transmitted through the structure to the interior spaces of the building. The building enclosure must cope with this, for example, by use of double glazing with a large air gap (around 100mm), sealing of holes and use of heavy materials.

It should be noted that the level of insulation is not the same across the frequency range. It is usually easier to keep out the higher frequencies of sound than the lower ones, as anyone who has lived next door to a rock music fan will know!

Maintenance and enclosure

Maintenance is dealt with in more depth in Chapter 8, but it is necessary here to stress some particular problems connected with the construction of the building fabric. Generally, maintenance problems with the fabric depend upon how much it is exposed to the elements. Eventually, many materials will lose their protective properties, but some are much more vulnerable than others and have a far shorter life. An example is bitumen felt on a flat roof, which has to be replaced regularly. An inspection schedule should be drawn up so that particularly vulnerable areas are examined frequently, and all areas at set periods.

It is well worth identifying particular trouble-spots. Examples may be hidden 'internal' gutters, exposed parapets, junctions between roof and wall, and changes of direction in the roof. In the case of gutters, for instance, inspection may pre-empt the catastrophic appearance of water through the ceiling. Making sure that leaves and other deposits are regularly removed by sweeping will help to eliminate this danger.

The effect of the sun should not be underestimated. Heating up of the parts of the building exposed to direct rays, particularly from the south, followed by cooling, leads to expansion and contraction of materials and subsequent cracking or rupture. In long runs of brickwork, regular expansion joints may be used. Flat roofs are particularly vulnerable, as has been noted, and once the waterproof covering is cracked, water can penetrate and damage the structure.

Deterioration of painted surfaces can also result from exposure to sunlight. Once such protective coatings are destroyed, the material covered is defenceless against other forms of attack and rot can set in in timber window frames, or rust in steel frames. A periodic programme should be instituted to ensure that all surfaces are protected.

Should joints pull apart due to differential expansion or the loss of elasticity of a jointing compound, then water will be able to enter the fabric and the downward spiral will begin. This is not simply a question of inconvenience caused by water penetration, but the final consequence is expensive long-term damage. Ultimately, if this process is unchecked, the structural members will lose their strength and failure will occur, resulting in collapse. Even a material as apparently tough as brickwork can easily fall prey to damage. If a parapet flashing fails or a gutter leaks then the brickwork will be continually soaked. During winter, hard frosts cause the water inside the brickwork to freeze. In doing so it expands and shatters the brick. The effect of frost on exposed, soft bricks, is very spectacular.

Chemical action is a special problem for metals used in the building fabric. Chemicals dissolved in rainwater can destroy the surface of structural members. Care should be taken to ascertain that exposed metal has a protective surface and that this is fully maintained.

Shrinkage of soil around foundations and settlement can lead to structural cracking which is not only serious in its own right but leaves the building vulnerable to further deterioration by the elements.

The above examples are by no means exhaustive, nor are they intended to be diagnostic. Simply, they point out the need for inspection and maintenance. It is usual for motor vehicles to be serviced at certain intervals and the very real prospect of accident or inconvenience due to breakdown means that these schedules are taken seriously. A building needs regular 'servicing' too. If problems are noted early on their effect can be minimised. Better still, regular maintenance can prevent these problems from occurring in the first place.

Exercises

1 Suggest a suitable structure for the construction of:
 a a student residence
 b a leisure pool
 c a 'bistro' style restaurant.

2 Describe, in as much detail as possible, the construction of the floors, walls, roofs and openings of two types of building operating within the hospitality industry.

3 Identify the insulation features of a hotel or catering outlet. Suggest a possible energy strategy for the same unit.

4 Undertake an external inspection of your place of work/study/accommodation. Report your findings suggesting reasons for any damage, fault or inefficiency. How might these be rectified?

4 Water

Objectives   After reading this chapter you should:

- Know how cold water is supplied to and distributed around a building.
- Know how water supply and storage is controlled.
- Understand the process of supplying hot water.
- Be aware of the variety of sanitary appliances likely to be used within the hospitality industry.
- Know the methods of removing waste water from a building and its surroundings.

Water is provided in most buildings to fulfill the basic human needs of drinking, cooking and washing. Additionally it is useful for cleaning the building itself, and may also be drawn off for the washing of clothes and for industrial processes. In the above instances, water is used directly, but it can also be used indirectly as a medium to transmit waste and heat.

Supply

A clean, pollution-free supply of water is fundamental to good health. The concept of directing water to many buildings, conveyed by pipe from a central source, is an ancient one, yet it was the increasing awareness of the need for hygiene coupled with the great expansion of urban areas, that gave rise to large-scale provision of piped water during the latter part of the nineteenth century.

Before then most households and public buildings relied upon private or communal wells. These often shared the same water table as nearby cesspits, and sewage leaked into drinking water. Cholera and typhoid epidemics were rife, and it is one of the advantages of the current system that water can be filtered and purified at professionally-controlled plants before being distributed to the public.

1   Source

Major reservoirs, located in catchment areas high in the hills, boreholes or rivers provide water for *service reservoirs* located near to centres of population. From here water is distributed through local *mains*. As described in Chapter 2, a statutory water authority is in charge of providing the supply and any new building can be connected via a *cold water service pipe* to the company main in the street. Whether a meter is provided at present depends upon the nature of the building, its size and use. In some counties all premises are equipped with meters and payment depends upon consumption.

In rural districts a public supply may be absent and private provision has to be made from a spring or a well, together with necessary filtration and purification equipment. There may be problems in providing a consistent supply all year round, as many springs dry up during summer. In addition, there may be a pollution risk from chemicals infiltrating from surrounding farmland.

2   Internal distribution

The way in which water is distributed around the building depends upon the use, size and complexity of the building. If the building has been designed as a whole from the outset, then the architect or services engineer will have considered a strategy which relates to the building's expected performance. Older buildings which have been reorganised, enlarged or extended over the years may well have systems resulting from a series of *ad hoc* solutions which are difficult to comprehend today.

3   Internal layout

Essentially, the layout of water services is a question of where to provide the supply, how to control it and how much of it is to be stored, as opposed to drawn off directly. Drinking water should come directly from the main, but water for washing or removing waste can come indirectly from a storage cistern (*see* Fig 4.1).

a   Supply

The advantages of an indirect supply are that:

- It guards against mains failure.
- It evens out the demand on the mains (e.g. early morning in a hotel when most sanitary appliances are being used).
- It reduces pressure on valves and controls.

The disadvantages are due to:

- The size and weight of storage facilities. These are usually positioned at a

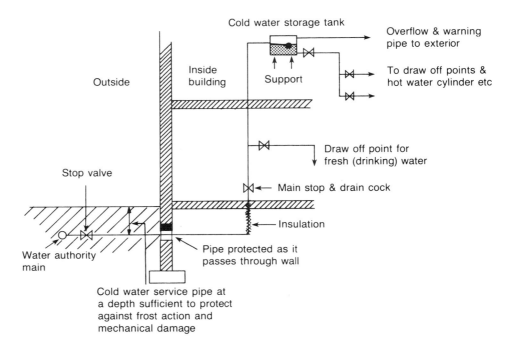

Fig 4.1 Diagram showing basic water supply

high point so that there is sufficient 'head' for water to reach all parts of the building.

- There is potential for contamination if cisterns are left uncovered.
- There is a danger of flooding if overflow precautions fail.

Access of mains water to the storage facility is usually controlled by a ball or float valve, which cuts off the supply automatically when a certain level is reached in the storage cistern. The operation of these valves is described below with reference to WC cisterns.

b Control

The first major control point is at the entrance to the premises where a stop-cock is provided. As can be seen from Fig 4.1, control points – cocks or valves, should be located so that branches or important appliances can be isolated from the system. This allows maintenance or replacement of appliances to take place without disrupting the whole system. Accommodation managers should familiarise themselves with the position and function of these valves, because any failure can produce dramatic and expensive results.

In tall buildings, booster pumps may be used to increase the 'head' of the rising main and force water to the top of the building where storage tanks are positioned, supplying floors with drinking water draw-off points on the way.

c Storage

Cold water storage is a strategic problem in building design. Galvanised steel or plastic cisterns are frequently used but, as water is relatively heavy and needs to be stored at a high point in order to optimise pressure difference or 'head', then the structure of the building must be able to cope. In larger buildings, service 'towers' may be taken up through the building and the storage facilities located in a housing above the roof top.

Water storage requirements can be calculated, based on figures deduced from research. This is a task best left to the services engineer but, as an indication, the volume of cold water storage to cover twenty-four hours interruption of supply is recommended at 135 litres per resident for hotels. Hot water storage should be allowed at about 45 litres per resident.

4 Pipes

Pipes used for water distribution are usually copper tubes, although galvanized steel rising mains may be employed. Increasingly, plastics are used, particularly for underground connection to the water authority's main. Lead pipes may be present in older buildings, but these can be dangerous, particularly in soft water areas, as lead dissolves and can cause poisoning of consumers. Water should be run off before consumption if it has been left to stand in the pipes for any length of time, irrespective of the material from which the pipe is made. In areas of hard water, i.e. those with dissolved limestone (calcium carbonate) in supplies, it is probably advisable to fit a water-softening device so that soap dissolves more easily and so that the build-up of calcium deposits in appliances used for heating water is prevented. Loss of efficiency and damage can occur if deposits are allowed to block pipework. Pipes should be protected from mechanical damage where they enter the building and where structural movement might cause fracture. They should also be protected from freezing. Water expands when frozen and ruptures pipe walls. Lagging must be used on pipes in vulnerable positions, e.g. roof spaces and external walls, to prevent this from happening.

Hot water

Hot water services are required for washing even in the simplest buildings. In cases where there is only one draw-off point (e.g. workshops), then an instantaneous water heater, akin to the old 'geyser', powered by gas or electricity, can be fed off the cold water supply directly at the point of use. However this is unsatisfactory when large quantities of hot water are required.

1 Storage

The size of a suitable hot water storage facility will depend upon the requirements for hot water and its pattern of use. For example, in the case of

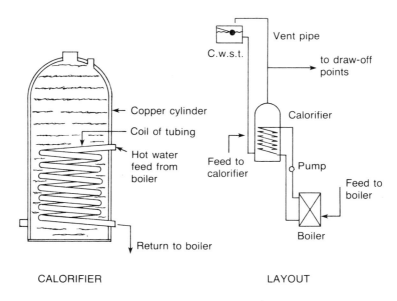

Fig 4.2   Section through a calorifier and diagrammatic layout

a hostel or hotel very large quantities of hot water will be required in the morning as people prepare for the day ahead. During the daytime itself and at night there will be relatively little call on the service and therefore the heating plant can operate over a long period. Less powerful plant is required than if it is limited to heating on demand (*see also* Chapter 5).

In most premises boilers are used to heat water for central heating and to provide water to be drawn off. Hot water produced directly by the boiler, however, is not consumed. In the *indirect hot water system* a '*calorifier*' is used and water intended for consumption is heated indirectly (*see* Fig 4.2).

The calorifier has its own water supply and is usually fitted with a thermostat, set at the maximum temperature of water to be supplied, which is connected to valves which control the flow of the heating water through the coil. The whole operation, of course, should be capable of being isolated, with valves to feeds.

In domestic scale accommodation the calorifier (copper hot water cylinder) and means of storage are one and the same. Usually an electric 'immersion heater' is provided so that supply may be maintained when the boiler is not operating. Non-storage calorifiers are akin to enlarged sections of pipe, containing heating tubes. In larger premises with zoned operational areas, direct gas-fired hot water storage units, consisting of a boiler and storage facility, can be employed. In addition, high pressure hot water may be used or steam. Water boils at 100°C at atmospheric pressure. When the pressure is increased, the boiling point is higher and thus more heat energy is available for transfer.

2 Supply

The hot water supply for domestic purposes is run from the storage vessel to the sinks and basins where it is to be drawn off. In the case of very long runs in large installations, a flow and return pipe may be used so that appliances towards the end of the run do not suffer from cooling, but are part of a flow circuit.

All of the pipework conveying hot water and the calorifier and storage vessels should be well insulated. There is little point in burning fuel to heat water if it is to be lost in transmission or storage before it is actually used. The glass fibre 'jacket' on the domestic storage cylinder is a good example of insulation.

Thus hot and cold water supplies are available for distribution around the building. Pipe runs are usually accommodated in the thickness of intermediate floors, or suspended ceilings. If they are run through concrete floor screeds then some sort of ducting with screw down cover plate can be used, so that should the system fail, easy access can be gained without breaking up the floor. In large buildings, service ducts are planned in, so that vertical distribution is readily accessible and neatly organised. Running pipes down and along walls is sometimes unavoidable, depending upon the position of draw-off points.

a Draw-off points

The type of apparatus used at the draw-off point will vary with the rate of flow required and type of operation expected. A conventional tap consists of a screw-down valve which when operated gradually increases or decreases the opening and the amount of water allowed through (*see* Fig 4.3). There is an appropriate spout to deliver the water. Rubber washers were commonly used to ensure a tight seal. Their failure leads to dripping, and nowadays ceramic discs are to be found.

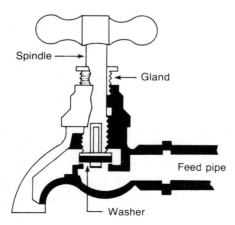

Fig 4.3 Section through a horizontally-fed tap

Manufacturers constantly seek to improve taps and there are many variants:

- bib taps are mounted against the surface of the wall
- pillar taps are used on sink units
- mixer taps where hot and cold supplies are controlled by separate valves, but water emerges through a common outlet
- taps which permit the replacement of washers without cutting off the water supply.

It is, of course, wise for the accommodation manager to locate the position of all stopcocks. When planning from new, it is important that stretches of pipework can be isolated so that repair work can take place without affecting the whole supply.

Sanitary appliances

As already noted, water may be drawn off for consumption at a sink or basin, or used to assist the passage of waste out of the building *en route* to the sewage works. The first stage in this process is via sanitary appliances. An extensive list of these could be drawn up because there are many types, and a range of materials is used. A convenient method is to put them into use categories as follows: sinks and basins; baths and showers; bidets; urinals and WCs; cleaner's closets, etc.

1 Sinks and basins

Sinks are used for cleaning objects (e.g. cooking and tableware, clothes) or for disposing of waste water from other cleaning or cooking operations. Wash-basins are used in the process of personal cleanliness.

In old buildings, stone sinks are sometimes still encountered and even those of wood with lead linings. Sinks made of glazed earthenware are still common. Ceramics of various types are now the most frequently used and have been popular for many years in the manufacture of a variety of sanitary appliances. The reasons for this are that ceramics produce smooth, rounded, joinless shapes which are easy to keep clean, and the glazed, non-porous surface is hygienic. The problems with ceramics are their weight, their vulnerability to chipping and cracking, and the need for a separate draining surface.

In order to reduce weight and to produce a strong and durable surface, integral sinks and drainers are nowadays made from pressed steel, either stainless steel which is self-finished, or ordinary steel which is enamelled. Unfortunately, the enamel is very vulnerable to chipping and stainless steel sinks and drainers are more popular. The integral nature of such sinks (single or double, with single or double drainers) means that joints between surfaces are minimised, thus reducing hygiene risks.

Wash-basins are usually made of porcelain as they are not subject to such

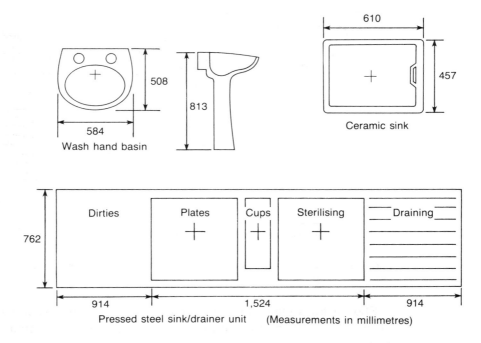

Fig 4.4   Typical wash basin and sink patterns

heavy use as sinks. It is an ideal material as it provides a smooth, sculptured, easy-to-clean surface. Where there is a danger of vandalism, stainless steel basins and sinks can be used, e.g. in public toilets.

A basin may be partially supported upon a pedestal of identical material, colour and style or wholly supported by steel brackets cantilevered out from the wall surface. In vanity units the basin is integral with a worktop (*see* Fig 4.4).

Cleaners' sinks are normally of glazed earthenware, mounted at a fairly low level with a bucket stand attached over the top of the sink.

2   Baths

Baths have, in the past, almost always been of metal because of their size. Early examples were of enamelled cast-irion, which proved to be extremely heavy, though long lasting if chipping could be avoided. More recently, enamelled pressed-steel which is comparatively light and strong has been used. Plastics are now extensively employed, particularly acrylic material and GRP, the advantages being that they are light, strong and 'warm' (the mass of a cast-iron bath takes heat from the water to warm itself). They are, however, vulnerable to scratching which may be a problem if an abrasive cleaning agent is employed by mistake. Most baths are panelled around their exterior to provide a neat, serviceable finish (*see* Fig 4.5).

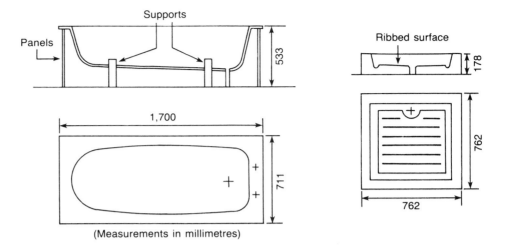

(Measurements in millimetres)

Fig 4.5   Typical pressed steel bath and acrylic sheet shower tray

Shower trays may be ceramic or plastic, with a ribbed surface to prevent slipping, a good lip to minimise accidental soaking of adjacent areas and an integral outlet (*see* Fig 4.5).

Baths, wash basins and sinks are usually fitted with an overflow arrangement, so that if neglected during filling, excess water will drain back into the waste pipe, rather than causing damage to carpets, ceilings etc. Should this become blocked through inadequate maintenance the results could be disproportionately expensive. Wash-basins are particularly vulnerable to blockage, as a mixture of waste soap and hair can form a formidable plug.

Special baths are manufactured for use in institutions catering for the disabled or infirm. Typically, the user can sit virtually upright instead of adopting the semi-recumbent posture which an ordinary bath requires.

3   Bidets

Bidets are provided in bathrooms for personal cleansing. They are made from ceramic material and may possess a spray connected to cold and hot supplies. Waste outlets on bidets and some wash basins are provided with a 'pop-up' waste controlled by a remote lever, instead of the simpler 'plug and chain' system. This obviates loss, and is more elegant in operation. The cost in terms of purchase and space allocated to bidets is often not justified when an assessment is made of their frequency of use.

4   WCs

Water closets linked to above ground drainage systems are the means by which human waste is removed from a building in the first instance. Before

(Measurements in millimetres)

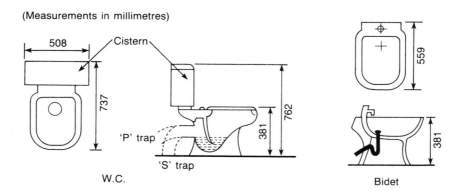

Fig 4.6 Plan and section of wash down WC and bidet

the era of mains sanitation, it was common for such waste to be carted away during the night for disposal, after removal from cesspit or ash pit. Today, nearly all permanent accommodation has a *water carriage system* for waste removal, whatever the ultimate destination of the waste.

The type of WC commonly in use in the United Kingdom, and that approved by water authorities, is the 'wash down' type and its variants. A ceramic 'pan' is provided with outlets to drainage systems. Water is maintained in the bottom of the pan. Above the pan is a cistern, filled with water, which can deliver a measured quantity when required (cisterns are usually of 9 or 13 litres capacity). *See* Fig 4.6 and 4.7.

In some European countries flushing valves are fitted to supply pipes, but these have the disadvantage that the WC is unflushable should the supply fail and that more water may be used than required. They are generally used

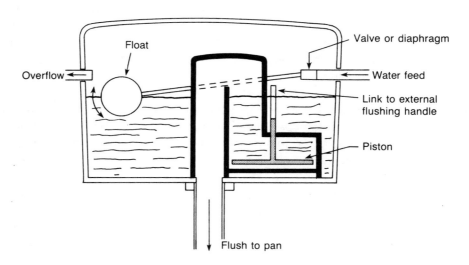

Fig 4.7 Section through a WC cistern

in conjunction with 'wash out' pans, which are shelved and lack the ability to contain water within their depth.

Should the ball or float valve in the cistern fail in any way (through sticking or diaphragm failure) then water will continue to pour into the cistern. For such an eventuality an overflow is obviously necessary and a 'warning pipe' is taken from above the water mark out from the cistern to the building's exterior. It is arranged to discharge where it will be noticed, i.e. near a door or a window, so that the valve can be repaired as soon as possible. The same principle applies to other water storage facilities.

Some WCs in higher price ranges have *syphonic* action where the flush is assisted by suction. The passage of water through the supply pipe from cistern to pan causes a vacuum in the pipe. If this pipe is linked to the WC outlet then the vacuum will assist the normal removal of waste effected by force of water. Syphonic WC suites are quieter and more effective in operation than conventional WCs.

5 Urinals

WCs are, of course, necessary to remove solid waste, but in buildings with high male occupancy, it is inefficient to use them for removal of liquid waste. In these cases urinals are supplied. In their simplest forms, they consist of a slab with a gutter below draining to an outlet and some sort of flushing system. There are variations on the theme. Slabs may be made of any suitable impervious material, e.g. porcelain or stainless steel, the advantages of which have been described.

Urinals bowls are increasingly popular because each has its own outlet and requires less building work than the slab type, the bowls being located on a wall and all drainage being easily fixed above floor level and run to a combined outlet (*see* Fig 4.8).

Urinals may be flushed at fixed intervals by use of a timer mechanism or there may be more sophisticated devices such as photoelectric cells set to either side of the slab. When the beam is broken by a user, flushing automatically takes place.

There are sanitary appliances for use in hospitals and related buildings which are too specialised to discuss in detail here. They follow the broad outline given in this chapter, even though some may be 'hybrids' based on different types, e.g. slop sinks.

Bathrooms (i.e. wash-hand basin, bath, WC, and possibly bidet) for hotels or hostels are usually considered as a suite of matching appliances.

Sinks in large kitchens are invariably part of schemes organised by various manufacturers of industrial kitchens. These specialists have a high level of knowledge about the operations which take place in establishments which have to cater for large numbers of people.

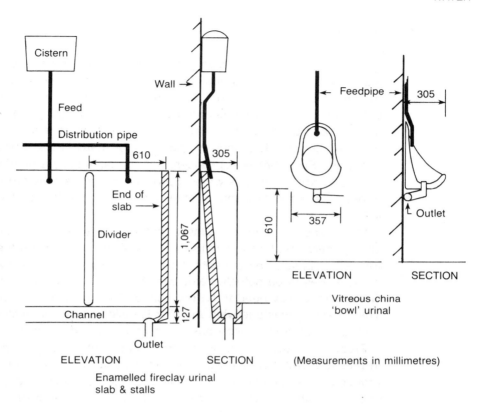

Fig 4.8 Diagrams of slab and bowl urinals

The water carriage system

Ultimately, the waste generated from sanitary appliances has to be transmitted to a disposal point. In urban areas this is the public sewage works operated by a regional water authority. In the country a public sewer may not be available and some private means of disposal must be contemplated, either a septic tank or cesspool. The system that operates inside the building is known as 'above ground drainage'. That which operates outside, *en route* to the public sewer, is 'below ground drainage', simply because it is more convenient to bury pipes to keep them out of the way, and, of course, to serve the low points in the building. If sanitary appliances occur in a building below the level of the public sewer, then some kind of collection chamber and pump must be used (with obvious problems associated with breakdown or failure of the electricity supply). There are also new systems of conveying waste through small bore pipes if appliances must be located in areas remote from the drainage run.

These problems are associated with old buildings or conversions. In new buildings the architect or services engineer will do all that is possible to group sanitary appliances, kitchens and bathrooms so that drainage runs are neat and efficient.

1 Above ground drainage

In essence, the idea of above ground drainage is simple: merely a series of plastic or cast-iron tubes down which waste matter travels by gravity, assisted by a flush of water if it is not itself liquid. Problems in design result from the behaviour of fluids in pipes and the necessity of keeping smells from the drains out of buildings. In order to tackle the latter, a simple method has been devised and has been in operation for many years. This is the 'water seal trap'. Fixed below appliances, it is fundamentally a bend in the pipework, which contains water. Sewer gases and smells are unable to travel through the water and cannot enter the building via the appliance (*see* Fig 4.9).

Most traps are formed in plastic, but use the essential 'P' and 'S' configuration. Bottle traps utilise a glass 'kilner' jar forming the body of the trap which is screwed beneath the sink. The glazed body allows the position of blockages to be detected and permits ready removal for cleaning-out. Grease traps may need to be positioned at a low level near to kitchen sinks. The grease in waste leaving the sink is solidified by cold water held in the trap and caught in a mesh basket which can be removed for cleaning.

Problems in traps occur when the rush of water along a pipe, or variations in pressure, perhaps caused by a sudden change in direction in the system, produce a loss of seal when the water in the trap is sucked out. Methods used to combat these problems form the basis for the system of drainage to be found in large buildings.

a The 'two-pipe system'

Here, waste from sinks and wash-hand basins is transmitted down one pipe; foul waste from WCs and urinals down another. If more than one appliance is located on branches of the system (e.g. in institutional buildings), then anti-syphonage and vent pipes are connected to traps to prevent the full discharge from one appliance from sucking the water from the traps of other appliances (*see* Fig 4.10).

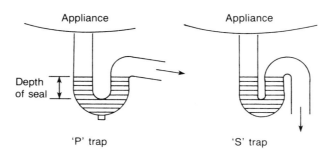

Fig 4.9 Traps to sanitary appliances ('p' and 's')

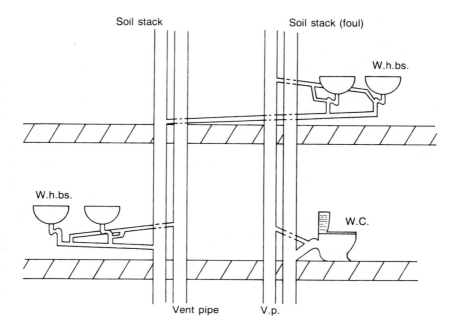

Fig 4.10 Diagrammatic section through a building showing the two-pipe system

b The 'one-pipe system'

This system uses a common soil stack for normal and foul drainage, but a separate vent pipe is used, as illustrated in Fig 4.11. This system has the advantage of reducing the amount of pipework, which can become very complex in a large building. The principle remains, however, to balance the pressure at the trap so that fluid rushing by from another appliance does not break the water seal.

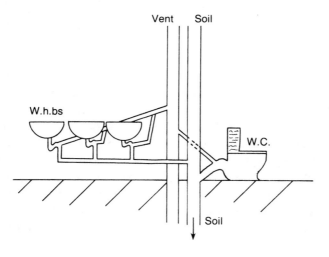

Fig 4.11 Diagrammatic section showing the one-pipe system

c The 'single stack'

This system may be used in smaller installations. Here, all discharge is into one vertical pipe or stack. Syphonage and blow back does not occur because gradients are carefully calculated and pipes sized so that large pressure changes are avoided. There are, though, limits on the number of appliances that can be fitted to one system, and the whole thing is restricted in terms of size. It is commonly used in modern domestic installations.

There are variations on these themes. Early systems are based on rules of thumb, but much research has been undertaken over the past few decades to ascertain the behaviour of waste in pipes, particularly in terms of pressure change and clogging and how pipe design can respond.

Any manager operating in a large or complex building should ascertain the position of horizontal and vertical runs, determine which system is in use and the function of each pipe, and note the location of access points. In modern buildings these will most likely be grouped and run through the building in service spaces or ducts.

2 Below ground drainage

Vertical soil stacks bend when they reach the bottom of the building, and begin their underground run. Too severe a bend can cause back pressure in the stack and blow traps on the system when discharge occurs. The main problems associated with underground drainage are to do with stranding of solids and damage to pipes. Should a pipe be at too steep or too shallow a gradient, then stranding of solids and blockage may occur. Liquid waste runs away too quickly leaving solid matter behind. The effect may well be cumulative. Badly designed and constructed junctions can also lead to build-up of solids. It is essential that access points are located where the system is vulnerable, that is at junctions of drains and at changes in direction. Such access points may vary, from 'rodding eyes' through to inspection chambers of various sizes.

Rodding eyes enable drain rods to be inserted into the pipe so that lengths can be cleared by the movement of the rods. Small inspection chambers, often of pre-formed plastic, relatively near the surface enable junctions to be inspected and cleared. Large chambers, or manholes, where drains are deep are of concrete or brick with footholds so that operatives can enter to clear the drain. Figure 4.12 illustrates the plan and section of a manhole.

Modern drainage systems avoid rigidity and are bedded in granular material to absorb some disturbance. Plastic and ceramic pipes now have flexible joints instead of cement to allow flexibility in the length of run. However, settlement or disturbance of the ground, or the running of heavy vehicles, may well crack or disrupt underground drains. In addition, covers to access points may or may not be suitable to take heavy loads. Vehicles driving on to pedestrian areas may disrupt covers. Managers should

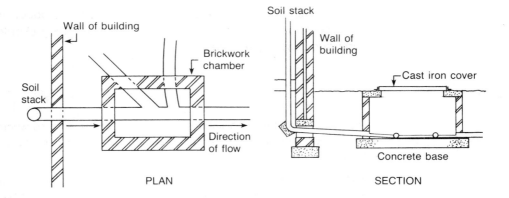

Fig 4.12 Plan and section of an inspection chamber

familiarise themselves with the location and direction of flow of outside drains and the position of major access points.

Managers should note whether the 'combined' or 'separate' system of drainage is employed by the water authority. In the former, rainwater drainage from the roofs, gutters and hard surface areas of the building runs in with foul drains, sharing a pipe. This may lead to overload of the system during a heavy downpour, although it is economical in terms of pipework. In the separate system, rainwater and foul drainage run in separate pipes. Partially separate systems allow some surface water to flush the foul drain.

Where no sewer is available, rainwater can be taken either to a water course such as a stream, river or canal, or else into a *soak away* in the grounds of the building. (This has to be planned in conjunction with the water authority.) If mains sewage is not available, which is quite likely in rural areas, then disposal of foul waste may take one of the following forms.

a Cesspit

This is merely a collection chamber, situated some distance from the building. It should be of an impervious nature, so that there is no leakage from the chamber into the ground, which could pollute water supplies. The cesspit needs to be sized depending upon the quantity of waste generated in the building and the frequency of emptying. It must be accessible to local authority vehicles which call to remove the waste at regular intervals.

b Septic tank

The septic tank acts to break down foul waste into harmless substances by exposing it first to those bacteria which operate in an airless environment, and then to those which act in air. The system thus comprises a tank into which waste can settle with minimum disturbance, and a second stage where there is maximum exposure to the air, achieved traditionally by spreading over a bed of granular broken stone. Septic tanks may be constructed by building contractors from brick and concrete or may be bought ready made as a package from drainage system manufacturers. They should be inspected regularly and properly maintained.

Exercises

1 Investigate the cold water distribution network within the building where you work or study and sleep and, with reference to Chapter 8, design an inspection procedure for its maintenance.

2 Identify the periods of peak hot water requirement at your place of work or study. Evaluate the methods used to supply the hot water and suggest possible improvements.

3 Analyse the cost of providing a hotel bathroom suite, considering each type of material available.

4 Investigate the system of waste removal used in
a a hotel built before 1950
b a residence built since 1950.
Describe any differences and explain why these occur.

5 Energy and environment

Objectives   After reading this chapter you should:

- Be aware of the various sources of energy supply available to the hospitality industry.
- Understand how electricity and gas are supplied to a building.
- Know the various methods of lighting, heating and ventilation available to a building services manager and how they can be controlled.
- Appreciate the various methods of increasing energy efficiency.

Sources of energy

1   Electricity

In the early years of supply, except in factories, electricity was primarily thought of as a clean and convenient method of lighting. From the 1930s onwards, however, the number of applications for electricity has increased considerably and recent rapid developments in the electronics industry have escalated the need for supply points in most premises. Labour-saving machines, food storage and cooking appliances, communication systems, information technology and computers and entertainment systems all require electricity in order to operate.

a   Distribution

Electricity generation in Great Britain is rationalised so that a number of strategically located power stations supply a 'national grid'. Demand can be variable across the country and the grid helps to even this out. Electricity can even be 'imported' from abroad if necessary, to supplement supplies in periods of excessive demand.

Distribution across the National Grid is at a very high voltage (usually 132 000 volts, but it can be up to 275kV or 400kV) as this is the most efficient means of transmission. Area undertakings distribute at 33kV, and this voltage is stepped down through a series of transformers and local sub-stations in order to serve areas and individual premises. Most non-industrial appliances in the UK operate at 240 volts, the voltage of the supply in domestic and smaller premises. Motors, machines, ovens etc. of greater than domestic power may operate at 415 volts and a 'three-phase' supply can be installed for the purpose. Large buildings with many fittings and appliances are sometimes provided with 11 000 volts and a transformer chamber is necessary in or near the building to handle voltage from the mains supply. Other nearby consumers can be served from this point.

Distribution within a building, of course, depends upon the size and layout of the building and the amount and type of electrical equipment to be used. By and large, as with water supply, certain principles apply whatever the scale of provision. These include the need to provide a *main service cable* to the premises from the public supply (usually underground in built-up areas), to distribute power to its points of use, and to provide means of isolating parts of the system. In addition, because electricity constitutes an immediate danger, there are also means of protection against surges of power, or electrocution through faulty equipment. Any work connected with the electricity supply should be undertaken by a qualified person. Mistakes and ignorance can lead to instantaneous death, injury or fire.

b Protection

This is provided by *fuses* or *circuit breakers*. If, for any reason, such as current running to earth from a faulty appliance, an excess of current occurs then the fuse wire melts or the circuit breaker opens, the electrical circuit no longer exists and supply ceases. Fuses are rated at a certain amount of current, and replacement by fuses of a higher rating or by some other electrical conductor can lead to danger or damaged equipment. Fuse links, fuse carriers and miniature circuit breakers are colour-coded for ease of identification.

Colours of replacement fuse links to British Standard 1362 are:
3 amp, red
5 amp, black
13 amp, brown
Fuse carriers and miniature circuit breakers are:
5 amp, white
15 amp, blue
20 amp, yellow
30 amp, red
45 amp, green
Care should be taken to keep abreast of standards and changing techniques in electrical supply.

decorative scheme, is used, and may be added to, so that a more specific message is conveyed. For example:

Gases are shown by a yellow ochre band
Oxygen has a white stripe added
Nitrous oxide a french blue stripe
Water a green band
Steam a silver grey band
Air a light blue band
Electrical services an orange band.

Environmental control

The major use for energy within buildings is to modify environmental conditions. These must respond to the activities that take place. At a fundamental level, it is necessary to produce an environment conducive to human comfort, and this is primarily achieved by attention to heating and ventilation. It is generally established that sitting rooms should be maintained at a temperature of around 21°C, that there should be air movement and air change enough to maintain freshness without causing draughts and that the amount of water vapour in the air – 'percentage saturation', or 'relative humidity' – should fall within the range of 30%–70% and typically be around 50%. In northern Europe, for much of the year, it is necessary to provide heating to achieve these conditions. In south east Asia, means of cooling and de-humidification are essential to satisfy these criteria.

Heating

In cool climates, nothing is more symbolic of settlement and civilisation than the pitched roof, offering protection, and the chimney indicating the hearth. Indeed, traditionally, the hearth is the centre of the home. Considered purely functionally, this form of localised heating is not a very satisfactory system. Fuel to be burned has to be:

- transported to the point of combustion
- temporarily stored nearby
- waste products of combustion must be removed both through a chimney and by collection after the fire has been extinguished.

Most heat produced in such a way either disappears up the chimney through convection or is radiated into the room, roasting the legs of those close by, but leaving cold corners in the more remote reaches of the room. There are advantages to a traditional fire, but these really only apply in a domestic situation. A large building with a variety of rooms would be a nightmare to service: solid fuel to be carried to each room on a regular basis, ash to be removed similarly, and a large number of flues and chimneys necessary to remove smoke. These latter produce building planning and constructional problems, as well as adding to cost. 'Local' heating, then, is problematic for large and complex buildings.

1 Central heating

The inconvenience of 'local' systems can be surmounted by burning all the fuel in one place, i.e. central heating, and the heat produced can be transmitted around the building by water, air or electric wiring.

a Water systems

The most common form of central heating uses water as the medium for heat transfer. This system has been widely used since the nineteenth century. In older installations, convection currents generate a 'natural' circulation through the system and large diameter pipes and heavy cast-iron radiators are employed. This system has several disadvantages, however:

- the planning of the system within the building has to take into account a boiler at the bottom of the layout and a natural path for convectional circulation
- pipes and radiators are heavy and use much heat to warm themselves before emitting heat to the surroundings
- the system is slow to respond
- pipes and radiators are bulky items.

In modern systems, small-bore or micro-bore tubes are used and a pump or accelerator propels water from the boiler and through the tubes into lightweight pressed metal panel radiators.

A simple central heating system is shown in Fig 5.3. This kind of system is relatively cheap, but has its faults, particularly as the last radiator receives water that has given out some of its heat already to other radiators. To counteract this, a 'two-pipe' system can be installed with separate feed and return pipes, as shown in Fig 5.4.

Given these basic principles, there is a variety of ways in which systems can be planned. These look logical in diagrammatic form, but in real life, of course, pipe runs have to conform to the structure and planning of the building. In small buildings, tubes feeding central heating radiators may run in the space between ceiling and floor, but in larger buildings zones are set aside for services and then 'local' distribution is along trunking.

b Air

Air can be used as a heat transfer medium instead of water, but it requires comparatively large tubes (trunking) through which to travel and a fan to drive it around, making it less than ideal in most buildings. It has a lower 'thermal capacity' than water and thus a greater volume is required to transmit an equivalent quantity of heat. It is, however, to be found in large buildings where air handling and air conditioning are employed to provide ventilation as well as heat and humidity control (*see also* the section on temperature).

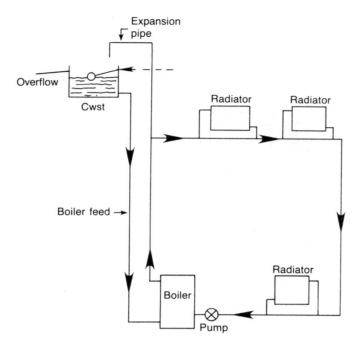

Fig 5.3   A simple hot water central heating system

2   Heat emitters

Panel radiators are familiar domestic appliances. The name, however, belies the fact that most heat is emitted by convection rather than radiation. Cold air is heated over the surface of the panel, rises, and is in turn replaced, thus distributing warmth through the room. The common practice of placing radiators beneath windows helps to counteract the cold down-draught found in these situations if double glazing is not provided. Reflective foil may be placed behind radiators on external walls to minimise heat loss.

Convectors are used in preference to radiators in some hot water heating systems. They consist of finned tubes carrying hot water, located in boxes

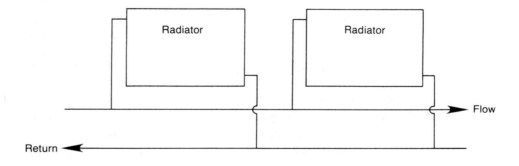

Fig 5.4   Principle of the two-pipe central heating system

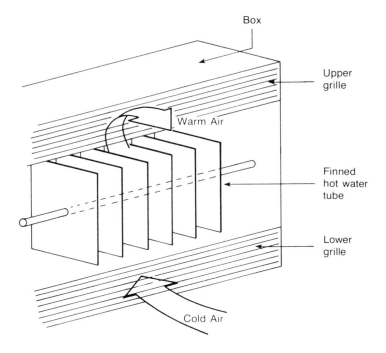

Fig 5.5   A simple, finned tube convector

with grilles at the top and bottom. Cold air is warmed, rises out through the
top grilles and is replaced by air drawn in at the bottom (*see* Fig 5.5).

In parts of a building where rapid warm-up is required, fan assisted units
can be employed, air being drawn at a relatively high rate over the hot water
coils and directed by louvres out into the parts of the room where it is most
beneficial.

There are other variations. For instance, coils of hot water tubing can be
located in solid floors and when the concrete floor slab is heated it becomes
itself a large radiator of heat. (This can also be achieved with electric cables.)
Problems can occur if control is insufficient and floor coverings become
overheated, leading to the discomfort of occupants.

Electricity can also be used as a fuel for heating. It is not subject to the
same constraints as solid fuel, gas and oil, in that it is very easy to transmit
directly and cleanly to each appliance and 'burns' without production of
waste gases. Consequently, small radiant heaters (electric fires), fan heaters
and oil-filled radiators plugged into convenient socket outlets are popular and
convenient portable sources of local heating. Electric underfloor heating has
been mentioned, and even heated ceilings may be found. Another form of
electric 'space' heating is provided by block storage heaters. These run from
cheap rate electricity generated at off-peak periods and charged separately.
Electrical heating elements are coiled between concrete blocks of high
thermal capacity. When the off-peak supply terminates, the blocks are left to
radiate heat.

3 Temperature

Temperature control is effected by a *thermostat*, coupled either to the boiler and pump or to a motorised mixer valve. Problems occur when the site selected for the thermostat is not representative of the needs of the building as a whole. If located in an entrance, for instance, constant influxes of cold air will mean that the boiler needs to fire several times to reach the set temperature. This would cause overheating in enclosed, well-insulated spaces. In larger buildings, it may be possible to install several radiator circuits, according to user or environmental zones, each operated by a thermostat appropriately located. Time switches could be employed to operate the system when required. Individual radiators may be controlled by motorised thermostatic valves.

In very large installations high pressure hot water may be employed to increase temperature. More heat is available for emission and losses on long lengths of transmission pipes and through emitters will not be so serious as with conventional systems. This system operates by boiling water at high pressure. Hot water 'mains' can then be fed from the boiler and distributed to all parts of a site or building complex. Local space heating and calorifier feeds are then taken off the main.

The services engineer will calculate the amount of heating plant required for any building, including both emitters and boilers, by looking at the standards required internally and by taking into account the heat loss from the building fabric. Cold does not enter a building unless in the form of draughts; the fabric *loses* heat, and the amount lost forms the basis for 'U' value calculations. Standards are now laid down in Building Regulations for the insulative properties of buildings (*see* Chapter 3).

There are legal maximum and minimum temperatures for working areas.

Ventilation

Some heat loss is due to air changes or ventilation. Air warmed within internal spaces is replaced by cold air drawn in from outside. Ventilation is absolutely essential to allow occupants to remain alert by introducing fresh, oxygenated air.

1 Natural ventilation

In the simplest situation this is achieved by the use of opening lights in windows to provide 'natural' ventilation. If windows are opened on either side of a room, air will flow between, provided there is a pressure difference across the building. In practice, most building fabric is very 'leaky', particularly where components join together and ventilation is thus assisted naturally. Building Regulations make provision for the ventilation of habitable rooms in dwellings, and for sanitary accommodation in all other premises, by specifying a minimum area of opening related to floor area.

Obviously, in larger buildings, or those with a deep plan, or in situations where openings would conflict with usage, natural ventilation is difficult to achieve or is unsuitable and some more sophisticated method must be used.

2 Mechanical ventilation

Mechanically assisted ventilation varies from the simple provision of an extractor fan, located, for example, in a kitchen wall, through to highly sophisticated air-conditioning systems. The extractor fan operates by drawing out hot, fume-laden air, which is replaced by leakage of clean, cold air into the space. In many cases, however, it is advisable to control replacement air both in terms of where it enters and its physical characteristics.

Components for a basic air handling system are:

- an intake unit
- a fan to move the air
- a trunking system to direct it to its point of use.

In practice, things are much more complex than this. An initial consideration at design stage is the amount of fresh air required according to use. British Standard *Code of Practice 3*, Chapter 1 gives recommended minimum rates of supply, for example:

- restaurants and canteens require 28 cubic metres of air per person per hour
- hospital operating theatres, 10 air changes per hour
- wards, 3 air changes per hour

By using data such as this the size of the fan and the capacity of ducting can be calculated. The amount and type of air handling required also has to be decided, and the degree of treatment to which incoming air is to be subjected.

Most air handling systems are organised with an input for fresh air away from any potential source of pollution and a separate set of duct runs to extract vitiated air. The position of inlet/extract grilles needs to relate to the design of the space to be serviced and its operation. What must be avoided is a layout where treated input air is directly attracted to the suction of the extract system. Figure 5.6 illustrates a basic air handling system.

A major problem at the design stage of a building is the planning of air handling ducts, i.e. trunking, and their integration into the overall scheme. In tall buildings, vertical runs are usually organised as common shafts, with branches taken off to each floor. Ducts are distributed across each level via a zone beneath the floor slab and above a suspended ceiling (*see* Chapter 7). Inlet and extract grilles are often positioned in the ceiling. In some cases, the extract is drawn out over light fittings, so that the heat produced by these can be removed when the space is too warm, or so that it can be taken back to the plant room and used to warm incoming air.

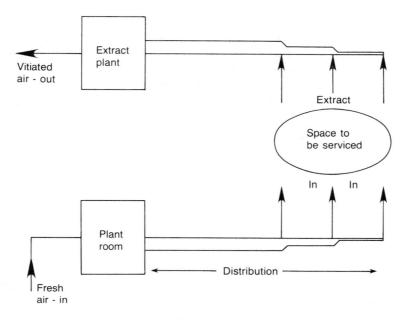

Fig 5.6   Diagram of a basic air-handling system

Incoming air can simply be filtered and taken into the building. In cold climates, however, air needs to be warmed and in hot climates, cooled, before circulation. In systems that are fully air-conditioned there is the capability to do both these things and to adjust the relative humidity (the amount of water vapour in the air). In south east Asia, where it is hot and sticky, reduction in temperature and lowering of relative humidity is necessary. In a north European winter, raising of temperature and avoidance of too much dryness is desirable. Figure 5.7 shows a basic air-conditioning plant.

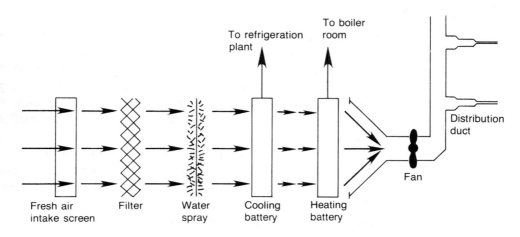

Fig 5.7   Components of a basic air conditioning plant

Boilers and refrigeration plant can be located remotely from the other elements of the air handling equipment. They are both heavy, and the boilers can be positioned in a separate boiler house. Refrigeration equipment can sit outside, perhaps on top of the building, providing the structure is conducive to this. Cooling towers may be used, as a great deal of heat has to be dissipated rapidly from powerful refrigeration plant. Much publicity has been given to the danger of disease associated with this type of installation and it is essential that all plant is cleaned and maintained in accordance with the manufacturers' and service engineers' suggestions.

Because air handling equipment is bulky and because in large buildings different areas have different requirements, air conditioning is often 'zoned'. This also means that equipment can be serviced or replaced without affecting the whole building. Neat 'packages' of plant are available, fed from central boiler house and refrigeration facilities.

On a much smaller scale, plug-in, or 'hole in the wall' air-conditioning units can be purchased for use in individual spaces. This may be a useful expedient, but air conditioning should really form part of an overall environmental strategy for a whole building.

Lighting

Of the five senses, the one most developed in human beings is that of vision. Without light we cannot see, and even the easiest of tasks presents problems. The principle of lighting buildings, therefore, relies upon providing enough light to perform tasks adequately ('task lighting') and upon qualitative factors. Our appreciation of spaces can be enhanced by lighting design, and signals can be given as to the purpose of rooms. A bright, evenly lit space suggests an efficient functional use. Rather dim, unevenly lit areas with a few highlights can indicate a relaxed atmosphere, desirable in, say, a restaurant.

1   Natural light

The quality and quantity of daylight entering a building must be carefully considered. However, it is by its very nature variable. The sun rises and sets, and the amount and quality of light changes between the morning and evening. The sun also moves its position during the day and, given skies that are fairly cloudless, may penetrate the building from different directions: *see* Fig 5.8 which indicates diagrammatically a building's orientation and the sun's path.

The diagram in Fig 5.8 is a rough approximation. The orientation of the building should have been considered by the architect at the design stage. There are also implications in terms of the action of the sun in heating the building (*see* the section on energy issues).

Daylight from the north is constant in the northern hemisphere. Windows facing in other directions allow for sun penetration and enable occupants subconsciously to note the passing of the day as well as adding cheer to a

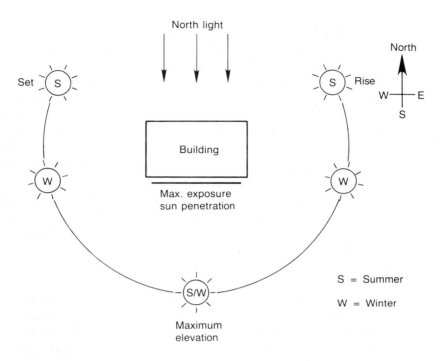

Fig 5.8 Building orientation and sun path (northern hemisphere)

room. In addition, it is psychologically important to provide 'visual release', or views out from the building.

2 Artificial lighting

Residential and leisure buildings are naturally expected to operate during non-daylight hours and the work place, too, continues to function long after the sun has set during the winter time. Artificial lighting is, therefore, vitally necessary. Indeed, in deep-plan buildings or for internal spaces it will need to be used during the day, even in buildings with glazed curtain walls.

a Design

The number of light fittings required for tasks can be determined by using information given in the Illuminating Engineering Society's code and by application of various formulae. 'Illumination', or the amount of light falling on to a surface, is the most significant criterion and is measured in *lux*. The IES code suggests the following levels:

kitchens – 500 lux
general offices – 500 lux
treatment rooms – 1000 lux
hotel public areas – 150 lux
hotel bars – 150 lux
badminton courts – 300 lux

Although this is a very small selection of examples, it can be seen how widely levels differ. The human eye is very accommodating and the iris opens or closes depending upon the quantity of light. Thus, the eye can see in a dimly-lit entrance hall of, say, 100 lux, or where a highly specialised task, such as a surgical operation, may require many thousands of lux.

Other factors are used in calculating the number and type of light fittings, and formulae include the 'maintenance factor', which is based on reduced light emission due to build-up of dirt and dust. In addition, there should be a sensitivity to atmosphere, that is, the aesthetic qualities of the building and such problems as colour rendering. The accommodation manager should realise, therefore, that the design of lighting installations is not a simple matter. Care must be taken when replacing fittings to make sure that they are appropriate and form part of the overall scheme. These matters are also discussed in Chapter 7.

b Light fittings

Tungsten filament lamps are the type most commonly found in domestic scale buildings. They operate by passing a current through a filament until it becomes so hot that it emits light. The chief disadvantage of this type of lamp is that it is relatively inefficient, using the electric current to produce a large quantity of heat as well as light. Its advantages are that very simple twist or screw-in fittings can be used, replacement is easy and the quality of light is fairly mellow.

Fluorescent lamps are much more efficient, but require switch and control gear which increases initial expense. The lamp consists of a glass tube filled with mercury vapour and when a current passes between the filaments located at either end, the ultraviolet radiation produced causes the phosphorous coating on the inside of the tube to glow. Much less heat is produced than with a tungsten lamp and more light is given out.

Fluorescent tubes are available to give different qualities of light in terms of the colour spectrum, for example 'cool white', 'warm white', and 'daylight'. These fittings are properly called 'luminaires' and are popularly available as 'single batten', or as twin luminaires. They can be fitted with diffusers of various patterns which scatter the light produced by the tubes and prevent the harshness and glare associated with naked tubes.

These are basic types and, of course, there are many variations. For instance, tungsten spotlights can be used on a track system to provide flexibility in the positioning of luminaires to highlight specific areas. These may be switched individually or controlled as a whole track. The bulbs themselves can be silvered, or reflective fittings can be used.

Dimmer switches with rotating control knobs act to increase or diminish light intensity from luminaires at will. In addition, various permutations of lamps may be controlled from a bank of switches. Two-way switches, common in domestic installations, enable a lamp to be controlled from either end of a corridor or stairway.

Specialist lighting is not covered here. Cinemas and theatres have complex installations outside the scope of this book. Multi-purpose spaces, pools and discotheques are similarly specialised.

Externally, high pressure sodium and tungsten halogen lamps are used for lighting access roads or general areas. These can be automatically switched on by photoelectric cells when darkness falls. For security purposes, switches may also be operated by intruder-sensing devices. Security and emergency lighting are covered in Chapter 6.

Energy issues

Buildings consume energy both in construction and use. It is the latter with which we are concerned here, though it is worth noting that on a global scale a building with a high proportion of steel, glass and aluminium will have used more of the earth's irreplaceable resources at the outset than one made from timber, irrespective of running cost.

In use, many buildings consume more energy than is necessary and this adds substantially to recurring expense. Savings can be made in three ways:

- by modifying user patterns within the existing building
- by spending capital sums to increase the energy efficiency of the building
- by spending capital sums to replace part of the conventional gas and electricity supply with mechanisms for using 'cheap' or free energy.

In the first case, little or no cash investment is required in order to effect savings, and this could be the starting point for any attempt to reduce fuel bills. Questions to be asked are:

Can the building be used more efficiently?
Are there any practices or habits which use fuel unnecessarily? (are entrance doors left open? are some spaces used infrequently and heated up only to be left to cool down?)

Costing exercises should be undertaken to see whether real savings are made, or whether capital outlay and interest charges exceed reductions in regular spending on fuel. This suggestion, of course, takes no account of broader environmental issues. (The Energy Technology Support Unit, which is part of the Energy Efficiency Office, commissioned two reports, in 1983 and 1986, which attempt to provide a greater awareness of energy costs in the hotel and catering industry.)

Increasing energy efficiency

In broad terms, in cold climates energy is used to heat the building fabric and air within the building. In hot climates it is used to cool down internal spaces. Initial efforts, therefore, should include an increase in thermal insulation of the building envelope. Part 'L' of the Building Regulations deals with this, and the need for good insulative standards was recognised after the energy crises of the early 1970s. (The relationship between building enclosure and thermal insulation is discussed in Chapter 3.) There is no reason why the requirements of the Building Regulations should not be exceeded, but if construction took place before about 1970 it may well be that they are not even met.

1 Insulation

All parts of an enclosure are important: walls, roofs, and floors. Insulating material such as glass fibre is obtainable in rolls for laying in roof spaces between joists. Wall insulation is more problematic. In the case of a new cavity wall, if loadbearing construction is used, solid sheets of plastic foam can be fixed against the outside of the inner leaf or foam-filled concrete blocks can be used. Where existing cavity walls have to be insulated there has been a practice of filling the cavity with polyurethane foam or blown granules. However, there has been trouble with foam in certain installations, where fumes have entered the building. In addition, hairline cracks can develop which encourage water to cross the cavity by capillary action. If cavity fill of any sort is used, then it is best to consult a specialist contractor with a good reputation.

Insulation can be externally applied, and there are systems available where it may be attached to the outer wall of a building and then rendered over. If insulation is wrongly positioned with regard to the construction there may be undesirable consequences. For instance, too rapid a cooling across the wall could lead to condensation actually within the structure. This, in turn, could cause serious deterioration.

Energy saving begins at a personal level. The need to heat is relative to our physical nature as warm-blooded creatures. Warm clothes which trap air are the first line of defence and the cheapest form of insulation. If a whole space is to be heated to 21°C – and in an ordinary sitting room there may be 50 cubic metres of air – it is important not to throw away the energy used for this heating. The building fabric itself must be a warm overcoat.

The most obviously vulnerable areas in a building envelope are windows. A thin layer of glass has very poor insulative properties. By double glazing, not only is an extra layer added, but the air space between enhances the insulative value. Unfortunately, the width of gap suitable for thermal purposes is not enough for effective acoustic insulation. Double glazing can be installed by the fitting of secondary frames with their own glazing, removable for cleaning, or by using factory sealed units. These need special frames. They can be coated with a film to reflect radiated heat back into the room.

These solutions to thermal problems apply to conventional construction. Those working in curtain-walled buildings built in the late 1950s may find that creative thinking is required to uprate the insulative properties of the envelope, and the advice of an architect should be sought. In all cases, though, whether small- or large-scale solutions are required, a cost and comfort exercise should be undertaken. It is difficult to quantify comfort, however, and better insulation may lead to under-used rooms becoming popular.

When building from new, energy and climatic issues should be taken into account by both client and architect and should influence the design. Planning so that the building is not exposed to the chill winds of the north, but opens itself out to the sunny south can be a first step. Careful control of the amount of glazing is essential, as is a good specification for a warm 'overcoat'.

2 Heat recovery

If there is to be mechanically assisted ventilation, then some form of heat recovery system could be used. Warm air to be extracted can be passed over a heat-exchanger (a device for transferring the heat from the air to some other medium, e.g. water, where it can be used more efficiently), so that the energy which has been expended in bringing it up to the correct temperature is not wasted. In addition, the extract air can be removed in such a way that it passes over light fittings and other heat producing appliances. The heat thus gained is then used to warm in-coming air via the heat exchanger.

In hot and humid parts of the world there is a move to study the ways in which traditional buildings work and to use the lessons learnt in providing modern accommodation which reinterprets traditional methods, rather than providing western buildings packed with air-conditioning equipment. This is an energy saving move as well as one of cultural significance.

3 Cheap energy

Unlike fossil fuels such as coal and oil, there are other forms of natural energy which are both free and constantly available; there is no store to be depleted. The main problem is that there are as yet few efficient means available to convert them into useable supplies. Sometimes, although the energy is initially free, the technology to make it useful is expensive.

Even when the air temperature is low, on a sunny day the energy to be 'caught' from the sun can be quite considerable. Unfortunately, most solar energy is available when demand is at a minimum. In other words, room heating is not really desirable on hot summer afternoons. However, there are two ways in which the sun's energy can be utilised easily:

- by storing or retaining the heat until it can be used
- by using the energy to heat water which is to be drawn off.

In the first case, the heat can be stored on a short- or long-term basis. In some climates, hot days may be followed by extremely cold nights. Even in the temperate climates of north west Europe clear days in autumn, winter and spring can have abundant sunshine and low air temperatures.

In the northern hemisphere, south-facing walls will be incident to the sun's rays and if the material from which they are composed has a high thermal capacity, heat will be absorbed and will be radiated out over a fairly long period, e.g. in the evening when it is cold. Similarly, any spaces behind south-facing windows will heat up and the air temperature can rise considerably. The air can be drawn off and passed over a heat exchanger. This is the case in long-term storage. A *rock store* can be located beneath the building and can be constantly warmed during the sunny parts of the year, either by blowing warm air over it, or by transferring the heat to water tubes, which then run through the store. It gives out its heat during winter.

4 Energy collecting devices

a Solar panels

These are a popular method of collecting the sun's energy because they are relatively easy to install. A south-facing pitched roof is an ideal location for a range of panels. Water tubes are sandwiched between the glazing of the panel and an absorbent surface. Water circulating through the tubes is heated and can be passed through a calorifier to warm water for drawing off. More often than not, because the temperature reached is not high, it will supplement supplies to the boiler and help to reduce heating costs. Solar panels are useful in hotels and hostels in particular, when, no matter how warm the weather, plenty of hot water is required for washing. In Great Britain, the installation of panels may require planning permission and wherever they are to be used, thought should be given to the aesthetic results of installation.

b Electricity

This can be generated by 'free' sources of energy. A small stream may have sufficient power to drive a turbine linked to an alternator which will produce enough electricity for a building or settlement. The motion of waves or tides is another possible source, though this is probably more suitable for large-scale operations. Windmills, long used as a source of mechanical power, are now used to generate electricity. Large-scale 'wind farms' exist in some areas, and a great deal of research has gone into suitable types of blades and blade configurations. Individual windmills, properly located, can play a considerable role in providing power efficiently. Even a low output windmill, however, is a comparatively large and obtrusive structure.

Historically, although sources such as small water-driven turbines have been used where no power supply has been available, there can be few areas in the UK now too far removed from the electricity network to need a separate generator. If this is the case, a diesel generator set is commonly employed.

In terms of 'free energy' the cost of the installation must be considered. In the case of a windmill, there will be building work for the foundations and pylon, the cost of the blades, rotor head and gearing and additionally, for control gear, switches and storage batteries. Added to this is maintenance.

Taken over a period of time costs per unit of electricity could be high. From the consumer's viewpoint a costing exercise should be undertaken, and it may be that 'free' electricity is more expensive than that purchased from the local electricity authority. Globally speaking, however, it seems essential that these free and clean resources are exploited.

Exercises

1 In conjunction with the building services manager discuss the type of electrical circuit which exists in the building where you work or study. Locate and identify its main elements (under supervision).

2 Analyse the tariff structures/costs of the various energy sources found within a patient care building. Assess the efficiency of each type of fuel used and suggest how possible savings could be made.

3 Identify the central heating system and its components which exist in a large hotel complex. Investigate any problems which frequently occur and suggest how they may be overcome.

4 Design a new lighting scheme, considering cost, for an area of a hospitality building with which you are familiar.

5 Investigate the measures you would take to improve the energy efficiency of a large hospitality or leisure complex in both the short and long term.

6 Circulation, security, communication

Objectives

After reading this chapter you should:

- Be aware of the various means available for enabling the efficient circulation of people, goods, documents and waste within a hospitality unit.
- Know the various types of fire fighting, security and communication equipment available to the accommodation manager/buildings manager.
- Appreciate how a building's services can be affected by an increase in fire fighting, security and communication requirements.

Introduction

Previous chapters have discussed the services necessary for healthy and comfortable habitation. There are also many other mechanical and electrical systems that play an important role in the functioning of various building types. These are concerned with:

- circulation
- the movement of people and objects
- communications
- security and protection
- cleaning
- waste disposal.

They all make life easier or more safe, and in some instances have revolutionised building provision. The development of the skyscraper is a prime example, for it depended upon the advent of the practical passenger lift. In the near future, electronic communications could change the whole nature of the workplace, and this has implications for the accommodation industry.

Circulation

Vertical stacking of accommodation requires specialised circulation systems. Where relatively small numbers of people need to be moved rapidly through several levels, the lift (elevator) is used. If a continuous flow of passengers is to be moved through a comparatively small vertical distance, escalators are employed. Up to four or five storeys staircases are feasible, but regular travel between ground and fourth floor is exhausting on foot, and stairs tend to become congested because of slow-moving individuals. With mechanical circulation, everyone can move at the same speed without effort.

1   Lifts

Although all lifts consist of the basic components of a car or platform moving within a vertical shaft of space, there are many variations possible in terms of type, grouping, use and control. These are appropriate to specific circumstances. Lifts in hotels may be required to move guests between floors: newcomers from an underground car park to reception and staff and goods between service zones. In a hospital, lifts for visitors and patients can be separated both in position, frequency, speed and size.

Provision of lifts is a specialised business which should be carefully considered if new accommodation is proposed. If changes in building use require more or fewer lifts or variations in speed and frequency then service engineers and manufacturers should be consulted. In terms of building design, it is desirable to group lifts together, both from a planning and structural point of view. In terms of planning, access spaces to vertical circulation are kept simple and straightforward by grouping; in structural terms, the lift shafts can provide strong 'spines' running vertically through the building and helping with general rigidity (see Fig 6.1).

Passenger lifts can vary in size and speed according to conditions. Speeds can be as low as 0.5 metres per second and as high as 7 metres per second. Sizes can vary from six- to twenty-four-person capacity in standard situations. Typical speeds for medium rise buildings would be between 1m and 1.6m per second; 2.5m per second would be regarded as 'high speed'.

The lift requires a shaft in which to run and a pit below, which allows the car to move down to the lowest point in the building, with buffers for over-run. Structural shafts and pits are of brick or concrete and are fitted with guides for the car and space for counterweights and cables. In traditional layouts, the machine room − for the motor traction gear and control equipment − is located at the head of the shaft and may be visible on the building's roof as illustrated in Fig 6.2.

Sizes of cars are determined by the number of passengers to be carried and the load capacity of the lift, e.g. 600kg (8 passengers). They are of steel frame construction with durable interior surfaces of pvc coated steel or enamelled panels, although there is no reason why a timber veneer finish should not be used in more luxurious accommodation. Doors are usually

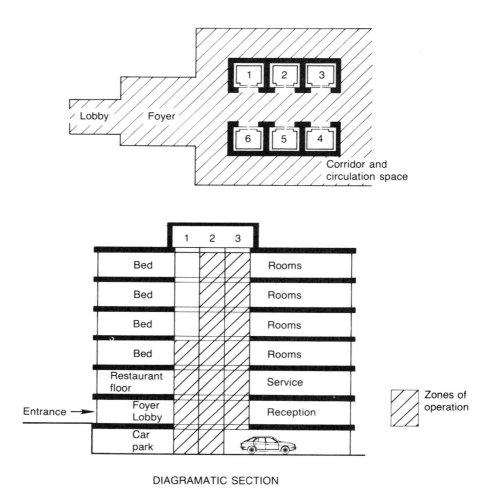

Fig 6.1 Plan of layout of typical hotel lift lobby and section through hotel

power operated today, and those with two-panel central opening allow speediest entry and exit. Electronic detectors or photocells are used to prevent the doors from closing on late arriving passengers. There would obviously be considerable danger if limbs became trapped in doors.

For complex or very high-rise buildings, control systems can be extremely sophisticated with banks of lifts operating on demand-based calls or call zones, or with specific distribution of cars between various floors. This allows for demands which vary from time to time (for instance, early morning rush-hour from lobby to particular office floors). It may be that a shuttle service could be provided from an underground access to reception in a hotel, or that floors with dining areas receive special attention at meal times. Sophistication in control gear also means that optimum lift speeds can be chosen between floors, depending on the stops requested. If acceleration is only up to, for example, 0.5m per second between adjacent floors, the

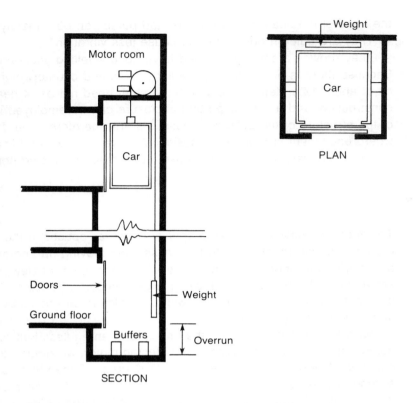

Fig 6.2   Diagrammatic section and plan of a lift shaft

deceleration time can be adjusted so that standardised slowing-down periods necessary from higher speeds are cut. This allows for quicker and smoother operation.

Most modern lifts dispense with gearing and have voltage controlled speed systems. This reduces vibration which is a problem in lift shafts.

There are several variations upon the theme of the conventional lift, ranging from dumb-waiters and mini-lifts required to carry food or documents, to large hospital bed lifts with capacities of up to 2500kg and doors at both sides of the car. There is an increasing vogue for glazed 'wall climbers' which are becoming commonplace in shopping centres. External wall climbing lifts present a changing feature of the Lloyd's building in London, where the lift both presents and is part of an aesthetic experience.

a   Hydraulic lifts

These may be more suitable than conventional layouts in particular places. Operation is by a piston, sliding in a cylinder, pushing the car directly or via a pulley system. Maximum travel is up to about 11m, and so hydraulic lifts are usually only found in low and medium-rise buildings. They do, however, have advantages over normal lifts:

– They minimise spatial requirements as no machine room is necessary at

the head of the shaft, and the motor and pump can be remotely located.
– They are quiet in operation and cause less vibration.
– They provide a smooth ride and have good levelling accuracy.
Because there is no need for a machine room and counterweights (though a pit of about 1.2m depth is required) the shaft need not be of heavy construction, and a self supporting enclosure can be employed independent of the structure of the building. These lifts are, therefore, ideal for situations where equipment is required in positions where none was originally planned – e.g. in conversion of a large house into a hotel or nursing home.

2 Escalators

Travel on an escalator can be a special event, as spaces in the building gradually unfold themselves to the passengers moving up and across from one platform to another. From a purely functional point of view, escalators are a very efficient means of moving large numbers of people over a constant period. Depending upon width, escalators can handle between 5000 and 8000 people per hour.

The machine itself works on the principle of an endless belt running over pulleys at either end, powered by an electric motor. Maximum rise is approximately 6m, at an angle of 30–35 degrees. Speed is around 0.5m per second and tread widths are 600, 800 and 1000mm. The main structure of the escalator – usually a steel truss – must be strong enough to span the proposed length, rather like an inclined bridge. Hand rails are driven at the same speed as the steps.

The steps need to be durable and nowadays are often made of aluminium, with stainless steel skirting. Escalator fires which have produced disastrous results have been exacerbated by the use of timber skirting. Awareness of fire, too, is necessary in the fixing of the escalator which, because of its inclination, requires a large hole in the upper floor through which to pass. Often fire shutters are provided over the top of the machine. In the case of escalators moving to different levels within one fire compartment, this problem does not arise. Figure 6.3 illustrates a diagrammatic section of the escalator.

3 Travellators and paternosters

Travellators are endless belts used where long distances have to be covered by pedestrians within sites, for example in airports. They are mainly used in flat conditions, although they can be used on inclines up to 12 degrees. Paternosters are designed for use in buildings where there is constant small-scale vertical circulation, such as libraries, schools and colleges. They consist of a series of small individual cars attached to endless belts. These are entered at each floor without any break in movement, and are obviously unsuitable for slow or disabled people. They are probably best confined to

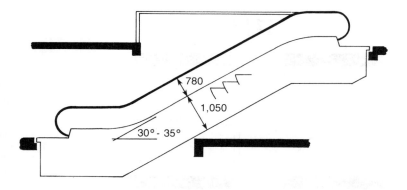

Fig 6.3 Section through an escalator

staff movement, where a constant number of regular users wish to travel from floor to floor within one institution.

4 Automated handling equipment

Complete systems can be installed where it is necessary to transmit objects through large or complicated buildings. Small container systems for use in hospitals, for instance, have capabilities for both vertical and horizontal movement, and whole networks can be set up (e.g. soiled linen conveyors). At a much smaller scale, messages, bills and receipts can be transmitted through vacuum tubes to a central station, e.g. the accounts department of a hotel, and returned to reception.

5 Waste disposal equipment

Rubbish generated in large buildings must be disposed of without becoming apparent in non-service zones. This is partly a matter of planning. Kitchens in hotels, for instance, should be near service yards so that food waste does not have to be carried through public areas. If there is vertical separation, *chutes* can be used to take waste or linen to a convenient disposal/collection point. At the base of the chute a *skip* or *hydraulic compactor*, which squeezes the rubbish into a small volume, enabling greater quantities to be stored, should be carefully positioned. Access is necessary for large service vehicles, of course, but if possible this should be remote from building users. The areas where chutes are fed and discharged should be easy to clean and maintain. The chutes themselves should be lined with washable, impervious material. Figure 6.4 shows a rubbish chute in section. *Grinders* can be located beneath sinks to consume rubbish, before being flushed away into the drainage system.

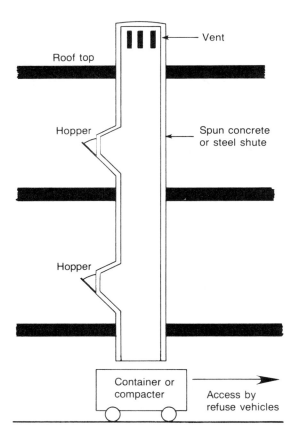

Fig 6.4 Section through a rubbish chute

6 Centralised dry suction system

This system is associated with the cleaning of the building itself and its contents. It consists of tubes or ducts built into the building, together with the other services. These tubes are attached to a central motor, so that extension pipes and heads can be 'plugged in' at selected points. This saves the transport of equipment within large buildings.

Mechanical circulation is an indispensable part of modern life in large buildings. The components are subject to much wear and tear, and regular maintenance is essential. Contracts are sometimes placed with the original suppliers or with small independent specialist firms. Whichever is chosen, the work undertaken is invaluable if it avoids loss of use of lifts or escalators for any length of time.

Fire protection

1 Fire detection and alarm equipment

The main danger to life in buildings is fire. The various precautions demanded by the Building Regulations and the 1971 Fire Precautions Act have been noted in other chapters of this book. The means by which fire may be detected and the ways in which it can be controlled are tackled here.

Fire detection cannot be left to the observations and subsequent actions of individuals. There must be provision of automatic detection apparatus. In large buildings the messages relayed from these have to be interpreted and co-ordinated. Electronically controlled detection systems can be installed, with information fed back to control points. In some cases, this involves a series of loops running to various zones in the building, each of which has a number of 'addresses'. Many hundreds of 'addresses' can be arranged to report back to the central control, so that appropriate action can be taken in terms of alarms, evacuation and fire-fighting tactics. It is even possible to produce a 'print out' stating where the fire started and giving details of spread. In this way modern electronics can be employed to enhance safety and information collection.

a Fire detectors

There are various types of detection equipment, but amongst the most popular is the *ionisation smoke detector*, which determines when smoke particles are present in the air. *Optical detectors* respond to smoky atmospheres, and *thermal detectors* sense a change in temperature. These may have built-in alarms and/or be connected to the control system. The positioning of the detectors must be carefully thought out so that false alarms are not given or conversely, that the detector is not slow in noting a real emergency.

Detectors should be chosen appropriate to their position. Smoke detectors located in lounge areas may constantly react to cigarette smoke, or they can respond inappropriately in a kitchen where grilling produces smoke. Similarly, heat detectors should not be placed near to heat emitters.

b Call points

There should also be provision of call points, i.e. break-glass alarm buttons, so that if fire is discovered at an early stage, warning can be given. In response to alarms, bells or horns can be used to sound a warning.

c Emergency lighting

In public buildings emergency lighting is installed, together with illuminated exit signs to guide occupants via a safe escape route into the open. In smoky atmospheres lighting is critically important, but it is essential to guard against any loss of mains supply and lack of light in internal spaces or during the hours of darkness. Emergency lighting is provided by specially designed luminaires powered by a battery supply. Batteries are stored on racks in a room designed for the purpose, and a control panel monitors performance. In most installations the batteries are trickle charged from the mains. Whilst emergency lighting may be 'on' in normal circumstances, some luminaires operate at only 10% of potential brightness.

2 Fire fighting equipment

a Fire extinguishers

Large buildings may be linked direct to the fire station, but there is every reason why early on-the-spot action should be undertaken to extinguish the fire or prevent its spread, provided the life of the firefighter is not endangered. There are also automatic systems which set about tackling a fire in its early stages.

Manual extinguishers are normally cylinders of 9 litres capacity which are wall-mounted in positions as advised by the fire officer. They are of various types and are suitable for tackling fires in accordance with certain categories.

- *Class A* fires of wood, paper and other similar combustible materials can be fought with water or soda/acid extinguishers. The soda/acid extinguisher, when deployed, mixes together ingredients which produce carbon dioxide and water. The build up of gas in the cylinder forces the contents of the extinguisher on to the blaze. The action of the gas and the liquid is to smother the flames. Modern extinguishers may be provided with gas cartridges (*see* Fig 6.5).
- *Class B* fires involve oil, spirits and fats for which foam, dry powder and carbon tetrachloride extinguishers are used.
- *Class C* involves risks concerning gases for which foam, carbon tetrachloride and multipurpose dry powder extinguishers are also used.
- *Classes D and E* cover inflammable metals and all fires where there is a danger of electrocution.

Fire extinguishers are colour-coded according to the extinguishing medium (BS 5423) – *see* Fig 8.4.

Dry powder extinguishers are versatile as they are non-conductive, non-toxic and non-staining. Clearly, then, the right kind of appliance must be positioned in the right place. When an emergency occurs the nearest extinguisher to hand will be seized and it must be the correct type, otherwise unnecessary damage or danger will occur.

b Fire blankets

Apart from hand-held extinguishers, fire blankets are useful, particularly for kitchen blazes where they can be dropped over fairly small but volatile fires. They are usually made of an insulating material such as glass fibre or even asbestos and should be sited near equipment such as a cooker or fryer. The blanket should be an appropriate size.

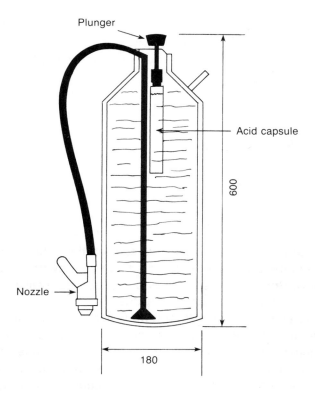

Fig 6.5   Section through a nine-litre water/CO_2 extinguisher

c   Hose reels

These should be well-sited. They can be recessed into a wall on a pivot mounting with flush fitting doors and swing out into use. This is valuable if they are liable to cause obstructions in corridors or are likely to be subject to abuse. The length of the reel should take into account the size of the area to be served and the position of other reels. Hoses are usually 19mm–25mm in diameter. Many hotels and multi-occupancy buildings have 'fire points' sited in identical areas on each floor as this reduces delay over locating the equipment in the event of a fire. It also enables the plumbing-in of hoses to be more efficiently designed.

d   Sprinklers

Sprinkler systems are available that require no first-hand intervention. For fires likely to occur in Class A areas, the well-established automatic sprinkler system is most commonly used. This consists of a series of pipes run at ceiling level over the area to be protected. A number of sprinkler heads located on the pipes are arranged in a grid pattern across the area. Figure 6.6 illustrates a typical sprinkler head.

Each sprinkler head is sealed by a glass bulb containing a liquid. When

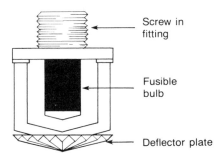

Screw in fitting

Fusible bulb

Deflector plate

Fig 6.6 A typical sprinkler head

the temperature rises the liquid expands causing the bulb to shatter, water then pours from the pipes and is deflected into a spray from deflector plates mounted below. Sprinklers are made of brass, but are available in various colours to fit in with interior design schemes.

Sprinkler systems can be fed from town water mains, but in some circumstances may require separate reservoirs and pumps. As with emergency generators for electricity, these pumps are connected to diesel engine sets which start automatically in the event of an emergency. Sprinkler pipework may be 'wet', in other words, always supplied with water, or can be 'dry' and only charged with water during use. Dry pipework is sometimes necessary in buildings which receive little heat during winter months and where there is a danger of freezing and bursts. The Fire Offices Association, which represents insurance companies, often allow premium reductions for premises with sprinklers. Unfortunately though, these devices can prove something of a blunt instrument and severe water damage can occur to premises, equipment and stock after, perhaps, a minor and easily controlled fire has set off the system.

e Gas emitters

For electrical fires and where damage to highly expensive machinery is likely, then devices for flooding zones with inert gas which will not support combustion can be installed. These operate best within ducts or in cable spaces beneath suspended and modular floors. Secure storage space for the pressurised gas must be provided.

f Doors

It is worth noting that fusible-link operated fire doors can be used at openings between compartments to avoid the spread of conflagration. In the simplest cases, steel doors of the appropriate rating are suspended on rollers adjacent to the opening. The rollers are located in inclined channels and should the fusible link operate, the door will roll across the opening.

Fusible links consist of metal strips soldered together which part when the solder melts at a pre-determined temperature. There are several variations on this theme, including guillotine shutters which fall across hatches leading between compartments.

Fusible links are also to be found in automatic smoke vents. Spring-loaded vents fixed in the roof are held shut by the link. Once it breaks the vent springs open. This allows the fumes, smoke and hot gases associated with the fire to escape, preventing the whole building from becoming filled with smoke.

There are many ways in which fire can be fought, and the correct warning device and appliance will depend upon specific circumstances. These precautions should prevent fire from taking hold and spreading. However, it cannot be stressed strongly enough that any planning with respect to fire, whether in a new or existing building, should be undertaken with the advice of the local fire officer who has first-hand experience of the effects of flames and smoke.

Security

It is not the purpose of this book to discuss methods of business organisation or even building planning to minimise criminal possibilities: there are too many variable factors. The crime prevention officer should be able to advise on security matters. However, as in the case of fire, modern electronic technology is capable of easing the security officer's burden. Remote controlled surveillance is possible from central consoles, for example, so that any internal or external areas of a building particularly vulnerable to crime can be monitored from closed-circuit television cameras. These cameras can operate in light levels as low as 2 lux and can zoom, pan and tilt. During darkness infra-red equipment can be used. The presence of a camera itself may act as a deterrent. Needless to say, other precautions like adequate lighting of external spaces can also prevent crime before it occurs.

1 Alarms

Should unauthorised entry to premises actually happen, then burglar alarm systems should notify both central security control, in the case of a large building, and the local police. The use of a siren or bell near the premises may have the added advantage of panicking the intruder into withdrawal. The alarms themselves can operate in various ways and, like fire alarms, the type most suitable for the specific location must be chosen, particularly to avoid false calls. Some operate upon the sensing of body heat: if a space is supposedly empty, any warm-blooded creature intruding will activate the system. Others guard potential access points by establishing electrical contact so that if a window or door is opened the contact is broken and the alarm is set off. Vibration sensors or pressure pads can also be used to activate alarms.

2 Locks

Restricted areas or rooms with valuable contents can be equipped with a variety of door locks to suit the particular situation. However, locks are often much stronger than the doors to which they are fitted. Remotely-controlled electric locks allowing access at the will of the person charged with security are commonplace, and digital and card key locks are particularly useful in buildings zoned for access by certain individuals. In the case of digital locks, a numerical code has to be punched in at a console at the point of access. The card key system is operated where a user has a plastic card issued by security, the electronic code of which operates the lock. Because of the coding system, it can be arranged that some users have access to all areas, others to a restricted number of areas.

Ordinary mechanical locks for operation with a key need to be considered for general low security use. To prevent casual intruders, it is probably best to use mortice deadlocks, set into the body of the door, rather than the once popular cylinder night latch which is located on the door face and can be easily smashed off or opened by those with no specific knowledge of burglary.

There is no doubt that a door itself is very vulnerable and any particular valuables should be guarded with grilles or reinforced shutters. A typical example is the roller grille drawn down at closing time over a bar serving alcoholic drinks.

Communication systems

In an age of increasingly sophisticated electronic hardware it is necessary to mention a few of the communication systems found in buildings which, if nothing else, require space for control points and trunking for wiring.

Modern telephone switchboards are available in various ranges of complexity and sophistication. Small exchanges may be positioned in large buildings and the range of their capabilities specified, in terms of storing calls, assisting transfer of calls, redialling engaged numbers and so on. Communications associated with telephone lines are now of great importance, e.g. FAX systems for the reproduction of documents, and 'modems' which are used to link computers and thus facilitate the transfer of information. Microcomputers and word processors are commonplace in nearly all administrative offices, whether for commercial concerns like hotels or in public facilities such as leisure centres. For 'stand alone' applications they need nothing more than an electrical socket. If they are 'networked', trunking for cables is necessary.

Entertainment systems in hotels and public address systems in large buildings need control points and trunking for wiring. Entertainment 'multiplexes' feed off to individual bedside radios or loudspeakers throughout the building. In hospitals, patients' remote call facilities must be 'plumbed in'.

Remote monitoring of fire detection and security systems can be combined with readout and computerised control of heating and ventilating facilities to give a fully integrated building management system, or BMS.

Exercises

1 Study the activities/movements of:

- a member of staff performing their duties
- a typical customer whilst on the premises
- linen
- restaurant bills

In each case identify the methods used to travel around the building. Suggest possible improvements in efficiency.

2 Locate all the fire fighting and prevention equipment at your place of work or study. Test its efficiency by organising a fire practice. Evaluate the results in terms of efficiency of equipment, and speed of evacuation. Suggest possible improvements.

3 Design a questionnaire to give to staff/customers/residents which will allow an assessment of their awareness of a building's security management. Assess the results.

7 Finishes

Objectives   After reading this chapter you should:

- Understand how the choice of internal surface can enhance the efficiency and aesthetic qualities of a building.
- Be aware of the range of finishes likely to be used for floors, walls and ceilings.
- Be aware of the various external finishes used to enhance the appearance of a building.
- Appreciate the need for protection of internal and external finishes.

Introduction

An understanding of structure and construction is essential to the accommodation manager, but it is the surface finishes of the building with which the manager is involved in regular day-to-day operation. Finishes provide protection to raw construction, add decoration and may be necessary for the adequate functioning of internal and external areas.

The naked carcass of a building is usually considered unsuitable as a background for everyday life. Although it may provide support, enclosure, insulation and all the other requirements discussed throughout the book, it can be undesirable from a more detailed viewpoint. For instance, a structural concrete floor, although perfectly capable of supporting its loads, may have an uneven, ridged surface. This could be dangerous, as occupants may trip and fall; it could create dusty and unpleasant conditions; it would be difficult to keep clean regularly or in the event of spillage, and it would not contribute to an appropriate atmosphere inside the building, unless the desire was for something perversely brutal. A suitable finish must therefore be applied. A specification for this finish could be drawn up, bearing in mind the following factors:

- amount of wear and tear envisaged
- strength and durability required
- degree of exposure to dampness or chemicals

- type and frequency of maintenance
- character and decorative requirements
- safety
- effect on environmental factors (in interiors, for instance, hard surfaces will reflect rather than absorb sound)
- capacity for protecting the building fabric.

External finishes, to a greater extent, provide protection to the fabric of the building from the elements, whereas internal finishes are more significant from the point of view of the well-being of occupants. In both cases, however, the finishes have decorative qualities which may even be the primary reason for their use. After all, the urge to decorate seems to be a deeply imbued human instinct. As redecoration is frequently undertaken, the intentions of the original designer must be carefully borne in mind. Detailed thought should be given to any new decorative finishes because the character of a building or a space within may be irrevocably altered and the value of a major asset diminished. Decoration is not something to be undertaken whimsically unless, of course, the building is a mere shell into which theme interiors are fitted every few years (*see* Chapter 8).

In the course of day-to-day running, the accommodation manager may be called upon to make decisions which affect the character of the interior. The choice of furniture, wall coverings and carpets is obviously important, but even minor details which come within the sphere of maintenance, such as the replacement of light fittings, may have significance when the combined effect of such small changes becomes apparent.

The character and use of space and its relationship with the rest of the building should be seriously considered before any decisions are made. There should be an overall image of the premises, and how any individual room forms part of the picture. The following factors are especially important.

1 Lighting

The way in which lighting is organised is of tremendous importance, because light is the chief medium through which we perceive space.

a Natural light

Consideration should be given to the quantity, quality and direction of natural light entering the building. Is there direct sunlight, or is there a flat, dispersed illumination from the north? Is light reflected from the ceilings and walls, or is the window contrasted harshly against the surrounding gloom? The questions of control by blinds and curtains and the reflectivity of internal surfaces are all related factors.

b Artificial light

This will have to be introduced to replace natural light during hours of darkness, but may be needed in any case to reinforce and supplement daylight. Illumination to enable basic tasks to be carried out is essential, but the highlighting of areas or features can enhance a room and increase its popularity.

Care must be taken to choose the most suitable type of light fitting or 'luminaire', so that the amount of light emitted is adequate for tasks to be performed, but also to create an appropriate ambience. Warm tones and colours are obviously more 'friendly' than harsh, direct light. (Reference should also be made to Chapter 5.)

2   Floor, wall and ceiling surfaces

The practical problems associated with these are well known to the accommodation manager and are dealt with here and in Chapter 8. Visual and tactile factors are also important. Initial thoughts may revolve around light reflectance, and whether this is of great consequence in the perception of the room. Colours should be chosen to harmonise or contrast with existing furnishings and fittings, and decisions must be made as to whether a warm or a cool colour scheme is required. If there are to be 'busy' textures and patterns, then these are best set against a neutral background. Surfaces or objects which compete visually can lead to severe cases of visual 'indigestion' and unease. A bland interior, on the other hand, can seem joyless and dispiriting.

Hard, cold surfaces can look and feel clinical, even if they are easy to clean! The luxurious feel of a deep pile carpet or the graininess of an old oak table can add to customer satisfaction.

3   Proportion

The relationship between the length, breadth and height of a room can be emphasised or played down. For example, a dark colour can lower a ceiling; a colour such as red will make a distant wall appear closer, whereas blue will make it recede. The picking out of horizontal lines will emphasise length. Thus, a brightly painted dado running along the length of a room will highlight this dimension, which may be very desirable if the room appears to be too short, or disastrous if it already looks like a tunnel. The stressing of transverse elements and banding may help in this case. It should be borne in mind, also, that various colour and lighting effects can put people off food, make them listless or evoke a variety of psychological and physiological responses.

In summary, the choice of finishes is critical not only from the practical point of view, but also because of feelings produced in the inhabitants. A whole venture's success may depend upon whether people feel happy where they are. When choosing internal finishes it is not good enough to adopt the philosophy of the leftover paint or 'make do and mend'.

Good quality is paramount in the case of external finishes, too. Initially, they represent a very small proportion of the building cost, but throughout the life of the building the expenditure on them will rise to a much higher proportion of overall cost. High initial expense with fewer replacements may be better value in the long run than early savings. The perils of neglect have already been mentioned in Chapter 3.

Internal finishes

1   Floors

It is impractical to mention the whole range of floor finishes that are available, without the production of an extensive reference chart. The aim here is to discuss principles. Manufacturers' information can be consulted to discover in detail the properties and performance data of particular materials and products.

If planning new work of any kind, it is important that structured thought should be given to the requirements of floor finishes at an early stage. A kitchen floor may be taken as an example, with significant criteria listed in random order:

- *Durability* has principal priority because kitchens are subject to heavy usage, particularly between certain pieces of equipment.
- *Safety* is of paramount importance because kitchens are potentially dangerous workplaces. Non-slip surfaces may be required.
- *Maintenance* should be straightforward and minimal. The kitchen is the 'engine-room' of many establishments concerned with hospitality and should not be put out of action.
- *Hygiene* must be easily maintained. The surface should not soak up spilt food or have grooves, joints or corners where particles can lodge.
- *Resistance*: the floor must not be liable to attack by hot liquids or chemicals.
- *Appearance* is important, as some people's working lives are spent in kitchens. The appearance needs to be fresh, pleasant and uplifting.

There may be more criteria not noted here, but similar checklists could be produced for any areas inside or outside buildings and prove of value in the choice of material.

Two or three finishes may emerge from this process as being suitable. It is then a matter of applying other criteria, such as cost, availability and ease of replacement in order to choose between them. When a material has been selected, e.g. quarry tiles, then final selection of colour and style can go ahead based on the ranges provided by various manufacturers. Repeat this process for every surface finish within a building and it can be seen that an enormous amount of work is involved.

When a new building is to be built or renovation is needed, the architect or designer will probably specify materials, but the accommodation manager can make life easier for the future by positive input and practical suggestions early on. Managers specifying new finishes in terms of remedial replacement work should, similarly, produce a list of criteria and select materials accordingly. Materials technology advances rapidly so it is advisable to check before choosing what seemed to be sensible last time. The following are the most commonly found floor finishes:

a Timber

In most instances the existing floor that will be encountered when considering a new finish will be of either wood or concrete. Timber suspended floors are common in domestic-scale construction or where spans between primary beams are broken down into small subsections. The 'walking surface' fixed by nails to the top of the joists is usually 'tongued and grooved' softwood boarding, or chipboard sheeting which is screwed to the joists (*see* Fig 7.1).

In some instances this may be regarded as an adequate final finish in its own right, and decorated and protected. In other words, it may be stained to give it a colour and then varnished or polished to protect it from wear and tear. It is only really suitable in this state for domestic situations, and even here, the preference of householders seems to be for a carpeted finish.

In most cases, then, even the 'working' finish is usually 'finished'. For example, a timber floor of softwood joists, given a surface of tongued and grooved boarding, may in turn be finished with carpet on underlay. Priorities would be given to decorative qualities and character, durability and ease of cleaning depending upon the intended location.

There is a similar hierarchy of finishes in the case of concrete floors. Rough constructional concrete is rarely suitable as a finish in its own right.

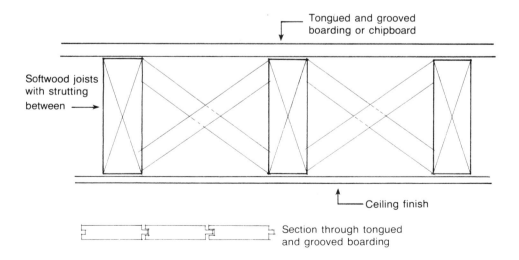

Fig 7.1 Traditional timber floor construction

Safety also plays a part. It is essential that wall finishes do not contribute to danger from fire, particularly in public places. Finishes are rated according to 'surface spread of flame' and conditions are laid down in the Building Regulations as to the desirable surface-spread grading in particular places. Obviously it is not desirable to use varnished panelling where vapours given off during a blaze cause fire to flash across and ignite the whole of a wall surface. (This is in addition to fire resistance which is concerned with the spread of fire from one 'compartment' to another.)

When specifying wall finishes the following criteria may be essential:

- durability, ease of cleaning and ease of replacement (fashions change)
- ease of repair
- character, colour, texture and reflectivity (is a bright, light-reflecting surface needed?)
- sound absorption (hard surfaces can reflect sound waves, leading to echoing effects)
- safety

It has been stated that some sort of finish to basic construction is required, but this is not always the case. The architect may decide to use 'fair faced' materials. For instance, an internal brickwork partition may be constructed in facing bricks which are then left bare as a finish. Fair faced concrete blockwork (which can be painted) is common and sometimes feature walls are made out of local stone. In refurbished or extended old buildings it may be that the existing stone or brickwork is left exposed deliberately to reinforce the character of the building and to emphasise its antiquity.

With new work, however, unless fair faced surfaces are deemed appropriate, in all but the most basic buildings a finish to cover 'raw' construction is normal. In the majority of situations plasterwork is used.

a Plaster

Gypsum plaster is normally specified and its use is beneficial in three ways:

- It helps to fill irregularities in the base surface and to provide a smooth level surface for painting or further finishes.
- It can improve the thermal insulation qualities of wall construction.
- It can increase the fire resistance of construction.

Plaster is applied 'wet' by a skilled tradesman and the number of layers used depends upon the evenness of the surface to which it is being applied. There is a system known as 'dry-lining', whereby plasterboard (a solid board with a plaster core surfaced with thick paper and made in 8' x 4' panels) is positioned against the wall on plaster dabs and nailed into position. The surface is then skimmed over with plaster after the joints have been filled and taped. This process is comparatively swift and eliminates a 'wet trade'. Partition walls which are non-loadbearing, are frequently composed of plasterboard on wooden studs (*see* Chapter 3).

In older buildings partitions may consist of timber frames covered with wooden 'laths' which are plastered over. The process of removing these or breaking through to make a new opening is extremely messy compared with modern partitions. Often proprietary systems of panelling or partitioning are used. These are sometimes 'self finished', perhaps with a vinyl surface. Solid partitions used in WCs and cloakrooms may be of chipboard with plastic laminate finish, which is easy to clean and is available in a variety of patterns and colours.

b Paint

Plasterwork can be painted with water-based emulsion paint, either matt or silk vinyls, as a final decorative finish or, once dry, decorated with wallpaper or other vinyl or paper finishes.

c Wallpaper

Wallpapers vary greatly in quality and price. Most is machine printed, but old 'hand blocked' wallpapers are sometimes reprinted for very special situations. Some wallpapers are 'washable', in other words they can be wiped down, but in most cases they should be used in locations where use will not dirty or damage them.

Surface textures vary. 'Anaglypta' has a high relief surface and flock papers have patterns produced by raised blown fibre. Hessian produces an interesting textured wall surface. Cork sheets and tiles may also be used to cover walls.

d Glazed tiles

These are commonly found as wall finishes in 'wet areas' such as kitchens and bathrooms. They are easy to clean and provided the joints are well grouted and the surface smooth and unbroken, they give a hygienic if somewhat clinical surface.

In the heyday of decorative ceramics, the late nineteenth century, painted and glazed tiles were employed in rather unusual locations such as public house interiors. (The refreshment room at the Victoria and Albert Museum is almost completely finished in the most surprising glazed ceramics.)

e Wooden panelling

This is associated with old buildings and gives a warm comfortable character to a room, perhaps even one full of antique overtones. Unfortunately, it is difficult to combine the desirability of panelling with fire safety considerations. Preservation of the appearance of the panelling, which after all is expensive, has to be reconciled with the need to treat it with an appropriate flame retardant.

3 Ceilings

The purpose of a ceiling is to add to the sense of enclosure in a room by concealing the roof structure and roof void. In addition, it can make

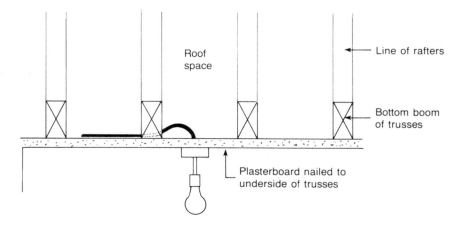

Fig 7.2   Traditional plasterboard ceiling

environmental management easier. Ceilings are sometimes deliberately omitted where it is thought desirable to use the roof structure as a design feature, for instance, in the case of old barns converted for other use.

The simplest form of ceiling consists essentially of plasterboard sheets fixed to joists running between the rafters of the roof, as shown in Fig 7.2. At the planar edges, where ceiling meets wall (or where apertures occur or even around light fittings) junctions have to be made with care so that if shrinkage or movement happens a cover strip or moulding will hide the gap.

In older buildings junctions and apertures are 'celebrated' with rich mouldings which are expensive to reproduce properly today but which may be valuable in enhancing the character of a room. Although they can be time-consuming to paint and keep clean, they form a visual feature which is of benefit. Care should be taken not to cut through them if new partitions are to be added.

The appearance of non-structural ceilings is limited only by the imagination of the designer and by cost limit, for example, the heavily coved and moulded ceilings to be found in old cinemas. Materials which are hazardous in the event of fire, however, must be avoided. Certain plastics can melt and drop in molten blobs onto the heads of victims, while other materials may encourage surface spread of flame.

a   Suspended ceilings

If a ceiling lower than the roof structure or upper floor slab is necessary to alter the proportions of a room, a suspended ceiling may be installed. Simple suspended ceilings can be constructed by building contractors from architects' designs, or more sophisticated proprietary systems purchased. These systems invariably consist of a grid of metal angles into which panels are fitted (*see* Fig 7.3).

Panels may be made out of flameproof material or pressed metal. Decorative effects can be obtained by choosing from a range of styles. Some

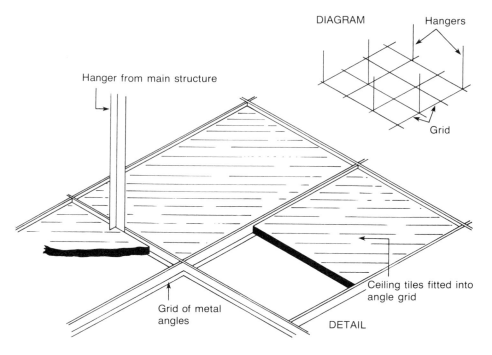

Fig 7.3 Basic proprietary suspended ceiling

Fig 7.4 Direction of space emphasised by ceiling design

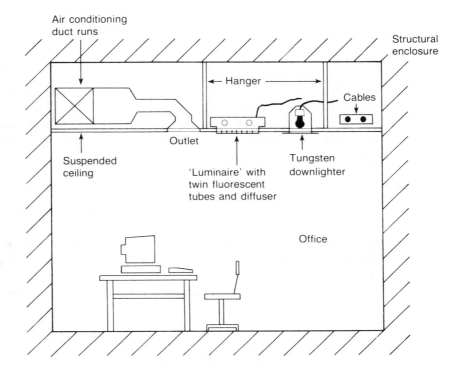

Fig 7.5 Diagrammatic section showing use of suspended ceiling to enable services' distribution

systems have long thin panels which can give 'direction' to a room, as shown in Fig 7.4. The space can be exaggerated in length or made to seem shorter and wider, depending upon the direction in which the panels are installed.

Suspended ceilings are extremely useful and are invariably found in large modern buildings where the structural floor to ceiling height of rooms is deliberately increased from normal so that services can be hidden behind the suspended ceiling (*see* Chapter 5 and Fig 7.5). This enables outlets from forced air ventilation systems to be located in the ceiling as a neat flush-fitting feature. Additionally, lighting fittings (luminaires) can be fitted into the suspended ceiling.

It can be argued that proprietary suspended ceilings contribute to the bland and faceless interiors of so many large modern buildings. Unfortunately, with such buildings, particularly those with a deep plan, it is necessary to accommodate heating and ventilating services as well as many light fittings in order to maintain levels of illumination far from windows. This may be best served by a neat ceiling system, particularly in cases where financial constraints are severe.

External finishes

1 Ground surfaces

Ground surfaces are often the first casualties of any financial cuts imposed during the design process. What may have started out as an interesting variety of finishes can end up as an even and depressing layer of tarmacadam. A good choice of external floor finishes can enhance a building greatly.

a Tarmacadam

Certainly, 'black top' is a serviceable and comparatively cheap choice, but although its smoothness and characterlessness may be fine for a surface on which to drive, it is completely lacking in any scale, textural or colour interest. The sight of any building for hospitality surrounded by a sea of tarmac should be avoided.

Choices that may be substituted depend upon location and purpose.

b Gravel

This is suitable for areas where there is little foot traffic. It provides a transition between grass and wall.

c Concrete flags

These are excellent hard-wearing surfaces, provided they are not subject to heavy point loads and are laid properly to avoid uneven settlement which may endanger the unwary. Their monotonous grey tones, however, should be varied with other finishes, though it is possible to obtain flags made with ground stone or coloured to give more life. Flags and all external surfaces should be laid to falls so that rainwater can drain off and minimise pooling and ice formation. Concrete flags can have ribbed surfaces to reduce accidents.

d Stone flags

These are infinitely more desirable aesthetically than concrete, but surface unevenness and varying porosity can encourage lichen growth and make them extremely treacherous if not regularly maintained.

e Brick paviors

These have a pleasant appearance, though they are rather costly. They can be laid in herringbone patterns and add a touch of scale and a variety of colour and texture.

f Perforated concrete blocks

These allow grass to grow through and are useful as they permit greenery to continue, whilst providing hard standing or vehicular access.

It is imperative that all external horizontal surfaces are not only strong enough to withstand the traffic envisaged – there should be no access to vehicles on concrete flag pavements laid for pedestrian use – but also to counteract the severity of the elements. Proper brick paviors or engineering bricks will withstand frost action. Edge a space with common bricks, and water will soak in. Frost action then splits and disintegrates the bricks as though they were wholemeal biscuit.

2 Walls

External walls are usually chosen so that the constructional finish is adequate aesthetically and is able to withstand the elements. In some cases, however, a finish has to be applied to cheap materials. An old building may require remedial work to prevent rain penetration or to minimise heat loss.

a Renderings

These are usually composed of a cement/lime/sand mix and are applied for purposes of weather resistance and appearance. A typical example may be where an adequate but unsightly concrete block wall has been used, or in the case of an old structure with an exposed gable wall where brick or stone is in danger of failing and water is soaking through.

Render is actually a traditional material in some localities, and provided it is well applied so that shrinkage cracks do not occur, and that its edges are well detailed so that it does not begin to break away, it will provide a serviceable finish. Variations are 'roughcast', achieved by adding small aggregate, or 'pebbledash', which textures what would otherwise be large areas of bland surface. A colourwash can be applied.

Rendered finishes should be checked regularly so that any early signs of deterioration, which are usually easy to spot, can be dealt with before large chunks of material start to fall from the walls.

b Ceramics

At various times in architectural history it has been fashionable to finish external walls with ceramic materials. Buildings from the last years of the nineteenth century and the early years of this century may have reddish-brown terracotta facings. The façades of public houses may be covered with decorative glazed tiles. In most cases these materials have survived well and the appearance of the building has been maintained. Dirt and soot washes off the smooth face, rather than discolouring the material. 'Thirties' cinemas are often faced with faience blocks, a smooth creamy coloured finish which also retains its appearance well.

There was a vogue in the 1960s for covering buildings with crisp, white tiling, a good finish in itself, but unsightly and dangerous results have ensued in various instances because of adhesion failures.

c Stone

It should be noted that in many modern buildings any stonework used externally is likely to be a mere veneer. This is easily seen in, for example, bank buildings, where marble or granite may be applied in relatively thin slabs to the construction beneath. These are excellent finishes for withstanding urban conditions but even financial institutions would find them prohibitively expensive for overall construction. More humble stones, however, are also used as veneers, particularly where a building has to fit into an existing stone-built environment.

In summary, any number of finishes may be suitable for external vertical surfaces. Whatever is chosen, though, must be in keeping with the character of the building and its surroundings. It should also fulfill the functional criteria of durability, ease of maintenance and ease of cleaning.

3 Roofs

Roof finishes have been discussed to some extent in Chapter 3. Generally speaking it is advantageous if they are lightweight, because this reduces the amount of structure necessary to support the finish.

a Slates and tiles

It has been noted that the small overlapping units associated with traditional pitched roofs are relatively heavy, but providing laps are maintained, they are long lasting and should be trouble-free. Because of junctions, they do need to drain quickly. In addition minimum pitches are recommended for different products and locations. Traditional Welsh slates, for instance, so common in nineteenth-century buildings, must be set at a steep angle of sometimes up to 45 degrees and laid in accordance with time-honoured practice to ensure that they are a reliable covering (though they do tend to delaminate with age). The same applies to ordinary clay tiles (40 degrees), but modern concrete interlocking tiles, which are fairly large and heavy, can be pitched down to about 19 degrees, depending upon the range used.

One frequently encountered difficulty in replacing broken tiles is matching colour. Pigments can fade through exposure to ultraviolet light. Modern, factory-made materials often do a good job of substituting natural stone or Welsh slates and they are usually less expensive, sometimes lighter and more predictable dimensionally, as well as being visually representative of the original material.

b Steel decking

Industrial buildings, and nowadays various institutional buildings, may be roofed with corrugated steel decking. This is relatively cheap, is available in large sheets and makes an effective lightweight surface. Originally intended for factories and warehouses and of a stark appearance, the visual quality has been gradually improved over the years by manufacturers who have extended both the profile and colour range. Bright, crisp and durable surfaces are possible and architects sometimes use the material in situations where once it would not have been thought appropriate.

c Membranes and sheets

'Flat' roofs in cheaper buildings, or in areas where they are unnoticed, are often covered either in asphalt or bitumen felt (*see* Chapter 3). Felt needs replacing periodically, and even if laid properly in three layers with a reflective stone chipping surface, may be subject to rupturing by expansion and contraction, or by persons gaining access and applying heavy point loads. Its appearance is usually poor. Asphalt, the alternative, is black and unsightly.

d Metal

Prestigious buildings may be roofed in metal, usually thin sheets of copper or lead. This is very expensive, but long-lasting and effective. Small areas of lead are used for junctions between roofs and walls (flashings), gutters and roofs, and over bay or oriel windows. Roofs entirely of lead are not often found, except in high quality ecclesiastical buildings. Copper roofing is more common, either for normally pitched or very low pitched roofs in prestige buildings. It turns green in colour after exposure to the elements unless some form of lacquer is applied. The texture of such roofs is smooth, but blandness is relieved by the fact that sheets are relatively small and the joints between units tend to break up the surface. In copper roofs, the welts and seams form a horizontal and vertical pattern and in lead roofs the 'rolls' are clearly visible.

It is possible to use a much cheaper, modern proprietary finish where very thin sheets of metal are bonded to a backing board which is then fixed to the roof structure.

In terms of maintenance it is essential that any restorative treatment to roofs respects the nature of the finish. Covering a tiled and slated roof with proprietary sealing compounds may lead to problems.

In discussing external finishes one of the prime considerations has been the need to keep water out. This is obvious in Great Britain and northern Europe. Not only may ingress of water destroy or harm the contents of a building, but, insidiously, it is likely to result in the deterioration of the structure through rot, corrosion or frost action. In other parts of the world this may not be a top priority. In the Middle East, for example, the main function of the roof is to shield occupants from the burning sun and insulate the interior. In other places rain dries out so quickly that attention to water resisting details is not critical.

Surface protection

Exposed timber and metal needs protection. Wood can decay, and fungal growth may occur if it is continually wet or if the fibres open up. Metals of various kinds are subject to chemical and electrolytic action, including oxidation, leading to corrosion and rusting. Paint is the main post-manufacture way of preventing this. Of course, steel may be galvanized, aluminium anodized and timber impregnated with preservative, but paint is a protective and decorative surface. Traditionally, primer, undercoat and finish paint (usually gloss) is used on exposed timberwork. The final gloss coat has a high proportion of varnish, and needs a good undercoat to provide a pigmented base.

There are many different kinds of paint, and manufacturers are constantly improving ranges. Paint for timber may be oil- or synthetic resin-based, whereas the emulsions used to coat internal walls are water-based. Whatever paint is used, it is essential to prepare and prime the surface well before using the undercoat and topcoats in the numbers recommended by the manufacturer.

Apart from gloss paint, timber can be stained and varnished. It is possible to obtain polyurethane varnish with a built-in stain.

In all cases painting should be carried out conscientiously and regularly. If not, the building will look unattractive and its components will be liable to deterioration. A painting schedule should be devised. It is usually cheaper and more convenient to do this than to replace window frames, barge boards and general external woodwork.

Brickwork can also be painted, although this is clearly undesirable on good quality facings. On poorer surfaces, cement paint may enhance appearance and protection. If water penetration occurs, then various synthetic resins can be painted on to the wall surface, however it may be advisable to subject the whole problem to close scrutiny as some other kind of remedy may be preferable.

Finally, special paints can be used to help in the event of fire. Structural steelwork must receive protection in certain circumstances to enable it to resist fire for a specified period of time, depending on its location and the use of the building. Intumescent paint is used to do this. When subjected to heat, it expands and provides a protective coating around the steel member. In use, it is thicker than normal paint, but expands to many times its thickness when the emergency occurs.

In conclusion, it should be remembered that the surface finish is of vital importance to the accommodation manager. It is the point of contact between building and user. Durability, ease of cleaning and ease of replacement must all be borne in mind. However, the chief functions are protection and decoration. If carried out badly both of these will suffer and money will be wasted. This is especially vital for commercial enterprises where the public has choice and will respond to a well-maintained and well-decorated environment, and will shy away from that which is unkempt.

Exercises

1 Suggest ways by which full use can be made of natural lighting in your place of work or study.

2 Carry out an inspection of the internal surfaces in one part of a building. Identify the methods used to finish these surfaces and how they in turn are protected.

3 Assess the external finishes of a hotel: ground, walls and roof. Suggest why they have been used and evaluate their success or failure. How might they be improved?

8 Maintaining the building

Objectives

After reading this chapter you should:

- Be aware of the need for and procedures involved in long-term planning for building maintenance.
- Know which areas of a building require regular maintenance and the frequency with which it should occur.
- Understand the dangers involved in failing to maintain a building and its services.
- Appreciate the importance of building hygiene.
- Know what equipment is needed to maintain a building and how it may be obtained.
- Be aware of the importance of efficient labour management within a maintenance department.

Long-term planning

The upkeep of a building used for hospitality depends chiefly on the work of two departments – housekeeping and maintenance. The organisation of these departments is largely dependent on the size of the establishment. It is only in large organisations that a maintenance department exists in its own right. Many small hotels, for example, deal with repairs, redecoration, servicing etc. in the off-peak periods, and many in fact close down and utilise their staff for cleaning and maintenance. They may also employ a 'handyman' or contractor to carry out major cleaning tasks and repair work.

To maintain a complex building, such as a hotel, efficiently, inter-departmental communication is vital. Each departmental manager should know exactly what he is responsible for maintaining, on a daily basis; how this is to be achieved, and where he needs to delegate to specialist staff. For example, the restaurant manager will ensure his staff vacuum daily but will liaise with the housekeeping department when shampooing carpets is necessary, and with the maintenance department if a carpet becomes frayed or starts to 'ruck up'.

Co-ordination is essential to ensure nothing is neglected, while at the same time allowance must be made for emergency repairs and major refurbishment, both in time and money. The person responsible for maintenance will therefore need to have a 'master plan' spanning between 5 to 10 years. This will have been prepared after discussion with the policy-makers of the establishment (directors, Board of Management, area/group managers etc.) and must be costed realistically.

One way of planning for the future development of an establishment is to undertake an exercise in lifecycle costing. This term encompasses the total economic cost of owning and operating a facility. It allows for an assessment of present and future costs and is a tool for making comparisons. It enables a realistic assessment to be made about the future effects of certain decision making.

There follow some examples of the factors likely to be considered or studied during this type of exercise.

■ Safety, reliability, operability. Environmental conditions may be more important than monetary savings.
■ Financial investment. The amount of money to be invested now to achieve a certain percentage in 'N' years' time through compound interest.
■ Land acquisition, re-designing existing assets, re-planning administrative structure, salvage from outdated or redundant assets.
■ Operating costs such as staffing, fuel, chemicals and supplies, outside services, transport, resource recovery, product availability, true money costs (state of sterling) etc.

Such an exercise, which can only be undertaken over a period of months rather than days, could result in greater expenditure than would otherwise have been the case initially, in order to capitalise on that investment. There are various examples: employment of an architect should result in better thought-out designs; more expensive equipment will last longer and reduce maintenance costs in the long term (double glazing); expanding facilities *before* they are essential may prove cheaper.

Maintenance costs have ultimately to be charged out to customers and so eat into profits. Good maintenance managers and housekeepers are therefore extremely valuable to any organisation.

Long-term planning should begin at the time when a building is commissioned. There are two stages to commissioning:

■ when the architect or builder is appointed to take responsibility for the erection of the building
■ when the building has been constructed and the management team take over the premises in order to plan the operation of the business for which it was erected.

Architects should automatically investigate the type of operation to be carried out in the building or complex of buildings which they are asked to design. This will help them to choose the most appropriate systems for providing water, heat, light, ventilation etc., as well as decor. They will have had to analyse the cost of every system chosen and this will take into account its minimum maintenance requirements.

After the second commissioning stage the person appointed to manage the building fabric and plant will have to become familiar with the brief produced by the architect so that they have a thorough understanding of how the building is to function. Unfortunately many maintenance managers are employed without this information being made available to them; thus certain economies built into the design can be mismanaged.

However, with or without this information, policy decisions must be made regarding the following points:

■ Labour (direct or contract)
■ Safety and security procedures
■ Inspection cycle for services and building fabric
■ The amounts to be written off in depreciation of the various items of plant and equipment
■ Periods of service for plant and equipment
■ Replacement policy for plant and equipment and furnishings: redecoration cycle
■ Financial planning for each of the above, i.e. budgets
■ Energy conservation
■ Training.

Labour

The number and type of staff employed in maintenance will depend on the company's attitude to 'doing-it-yourself'. A large organisation will usually employ a maintenance manager with an engineering background, who will usually have an understanding of plant operation and an appreciation of the skills required to maintain services, equipment and the building fabric. Specialist contractors may then be employed to supplement areas in which fulltime staff are not sufficiently skilled, e.g. electrical installations, plumbing, painting/decorating, joinery, gardening etc., or where specialist equipment or tools are required. In many cases fulltime staff will be willing 'all-rounders' as there is rarely sufficient work in one skill to keep a specialist employed all the year round. Employing direct labour will involve some considerable administration on behalf of the manager such as:

■ the preparation of duty rotas
■ the issuing, receiving and checking of time sheets
■ recruitment and all that that involves, e.g. advertising, interviewing, assessment
■ pay negotiations
■ union liaison rota.

However, their availability can be extremely useful during possible emergency breakdowns and malfunctions, and a degree of loyalty can be fostered, which often promotes a high standard of workmanship.

The employment of contractors also involves the maintenance manager in certain administrative duties but this will be more sporadic, such as once a year or even once every two or three years. This task entails:

- Obtaining quotes from individual specialist companies or general building contractors if a variety of skills is involved.
- Defining clearly the details of the work to be done for the agreed price.
- Negotiating for discounts and agreeing quick payment terms for work carried out within agreed time limits.

Once these tasks are carried out, all the manager must do is ensure continuous supervision while the work is carried out and pay the bill promptly, after thoroughly checking the work. Supervision of work and the hours put in by both contractors and employed staff must occur if standards and value for money are to be attained. It is also important to ensure that:

- no breach of the Health and Safety at Work Act occurs
- contracted-in staff are made aware of any security arrangements operated by the company and of the fire procedure in the area in which they are working
- security staff are informed of the whereabouts of these staff and the approximate numbers on the premises at any one time.

A maintenance manager should try to build up a good relationship with contract companies as they have advantages:

- They should be up to date with the latest technology and therefore perform the task efficiently.
- They may pass on to the maintenance manager their assessment of the general condition of the item they are working on, or the area in which they are performing their work.
- It is easy to quantify maintenance work if an invoice can be attached to the work carried out.

There are many examples of work carried out by contracted-in staff:

- painting and decorating
- floor sealing and stripping
- servicing and repair of plant, equipment, heating and air-conditioning systems, appliances and specialist machinery
- roof inspections and repairs
- maintenance of internal and external drainage
- maintenance of firefighting equipment
- general internal cleaning
- window cleaning.

Safety and security

The management of any building linked to the hospitality industry should have a safety policy. This should be in writing, and be seen to be implemented. This implementation is the responsibility of a safety officer or any member of management who has been assigned such a title. This may be the housekeeper, security officer, head porter or the maintenance manager, as the nature of these jobs provides a working knowledge of most areas of the building.

A safety policy is specific to an establishment and its complexity will depend on the size and nature of the building and the type of business. It will cover the following areas:

Health and Safety
Accident Prevention
Training
Accident Investigation Procedure
The use of dangerous machinery
First Aid
Fire Prevention
Personal Liability
Policy Review Procedure

Safety of a building depends to a large extent on the diligence of all grades of staff. It is therefore important that an induction programme should include hazard spotting and training in accident awareness, as well as instruction and supervision of safe working practices. 'Staff' should include contracted-in staff, particularly as their loyalties are likely to be less strong than those on the payroll. In such cases the managers responsible for employing them should decide how they pass on the importance of safety, e.g. safety signs, safety booklets, circulars etc. For all staff, however, such training should be supported by adequate supervision and when necessary, re-training sessions. These training sessions could take the form of a safety audit in which all grades of staff could become involved, including contractors (*see* Fig 8.1).

1 Safety policy

A safety policy must make provision for the following:

a The health, safety and welfare of persons at work, i.e. provision of protective clothing and safe equipment.

b The protection of others from risks arising from work premises or activities, e.g. use of warning signs, ventilation when painting, control of noise.

c The safe storage of toxic and inflammable substances such as paint, varnish, pesticides, fungicides.

Safety audit check list

	Yes/No
A. ENTRANCE HALLS, STAIRCASES AND PASSAGES	
1. Are the fire stop doors in good condition, kept in operating position and unobstructed?	
2. Are the lights adequate and in working order?	
3. Are all escape routes free of obstruction and clearly identified?	
4. Do escape doors open easily and are they identified?	
5. Are fire alarm operating points unobstructed?	
6. Is the fire fighting equipment all in position, unobstructed and without visible damage? Will it suffice?	
7. Are all floors kept clean and dry?	
8. Are all electric flexes, leads, plugs, switches and sockets without visible damage and in proper working order?	
9. Are lifts functioning properly and inspected regularly?	
B. PUBLIC ROOMS AND RESTAURANTS	
1. Are the work areas and escape routes kept clear and free from rubbish and obstructions?	
2. Do escape doors open easily and are they clearly identified?	
3. Is all the fire fighting equipment in position?	
4. Are all lights adequate and in working order?	
5. Are fire alarm points unobstructed?	
6. Are floor finishes kept clean and dry, especially in service areas?	
7. Are materials stored so as to be tidy and not liable to fall on people?	
8. Are all electric flexes, leads, plugs, sockets and switches without visible damage and in proper working order?	
9. Is a metal closable container provided to hold floor sweepings and contents of ash trays?	
10. Are fires (gas, electric or coal) all adequately protected?	
11. Are all service pipes/cables protected and not exposed to damage?	
12. Is the service hoist working properly and inspected regularly?	
C. TOILETS	
1. Are all appliances kept clean and undamaged?	
2. Are all doors, locks and catches in sound working order?	
3. Is there a supply of soap (or equivalent), towels and toilet rolls?	
4. Are extract fans (if any) in sound working order?	
5. Are all lights in order?	
6. Are used paper towel steel bins emptied regularly?	
D. KITCHENS	
1. Is the lighting adequate?	
2. Is the ventilation adequate?	
3. Is the water supply adequate?	
4. Are the floors kept clean and dry?	
5. Is there any equipment not working properly?	
6. Are there guards on dangerous machines?	
7. Is rubbish stored in suitable bins with well fitting lids and emptied regularly?	
8. Is the fire fighting equipment all in position, unobstructed and clearly identified?	

continued on p 140

Fig 8.1 Safety audit checklist – example (Courtesy of the Hotel and Catering Training Board)

Safety audit check list (cont.)

	Yes/No
9. Are notices on display? e.g. no smoking, fire use of machinery wash your hands	
10. Are knives stored correctly?	
11. Do the staff wear suitable protective clothing?	
12. Is food stored correctly?	
13. Is any food exposed or left standing?	
14. Are soap, nail brush and clean towels available at each wash hand basin?	
15. Are all surfaces undamaged, clean and free from grease?	
16. Is there any grease build-up on cooking equipment?	
17. Is there any evidence of vermin or insects?	
18. Are chemical cleaning agents stored properly in a lockable cupboard?	
19. Is the temperature reasonable?	

E. CELLARS AND BEERSTORES

	Yes/No
1. Are all lights adequate and in working order?	
2. Is the area kept free of all combustible rubbish?	
3. Are all goods stored so as to be tidy, not obstruct floor or exits and not liable to fall on people?	
4. Are all CO_2 cylinders safely secured – (small and large, full and empty)?	
5. Are all dangerous parts of machines adequately guarded?	
6. Are all flexes, leads, plugs, sockets and switches without visible damage and in proper working order?	
7. Any broken manhole covers or missing screws from double seal covers?	
8. Are vent grills clear and adjustable devices workable?	

F. BEDROOMS – GUEST AND STAFF

	Yes/No
1. Are all lights adequate and in order?	
2. Are all baths, wash basins, showers, toilets, etc., in working order?	
3. Are all floor finishes kept clean and dry?	
4. Are gas or electric fires adequately safeguarded?	
5. Are all service pipes/cables protected and not exposed to damage?	
6. Are all flexes, leads, plugs, switches and sockets without visible damage and in proper working order?	
7. Are TV sets disconnected from electricity supply when not in use – and notices displayed urging this to be done?	
8. Are fire procedure notices prominently displayed?	
9. Are electric kettles (where provided) in good condition and safe to use?	

G. EXTERNAL – INCLUDING OUTBUILDINGS, CAR PARKS, GROUNDS, ETC.

	Yes/No
1. Are lights adequate, clean and in working order?	
2. Are lights well sited to safeguard employees and public?	
3. Any broken manhole covers, pavement glass lights or missing gulley grates?	
4. Are any drains or gullies choked?	
5. Is there any accumulation of obstructive or combustible rubbish?	
6. Are adequate steel bins, with lids, provided to contain rubbish till disposed of?	
7. Is access to and egress from the building being kept unobstructed?	

When designing a building, extension or conversion, much thought and expense is put into the prevention of fire, and its containment if it does occur. This is supported by the provision of firefighting equipment and the development of evacuation procedures. However, all will have been to no avail if essential elements of the master fire prevention plan are tampered with, e.g. if fire doors are left open, a hole is created in the 'compartment'. If fire extinguishers are left empty or removed the ratio of firefighting equipment to area of building is increased. If fire exits are blocked an escape route is restricted, thus reducing the speed with which the building can be evacuated. Figure 8.3 provides a summary of fire extinguishers, and Fig 8.4 a fire prevention checklist.

It is very important that members of general management are aware of the

---

Fire prevention check list

CONTINUOUS MONITORING

Inspection of all vacant rooms last thing at night to ensure that all cigarettes have been extinguished and all electrical and gas appliances have been switched off and unplugged.

Provision of plenty of large ash trays in all public rooms.

Guarding of open fires.

Positioning of portable heating appliances safely away from furniture and furnishings.

Keeping fire doors closed and ensuring that fire exits are never blocked and are kept unlocked.

Checking that the emergency lighting is functioning correctly and that the escape routes are adequately lit (to be inspected every evening).

Keeping steps of external stairways and passages and balconies, which form part of an escape route, free from all obstructions and tripping hazards including storage, growing vegetation, snow and ice, washing lines.

Ensuring that communication equipment (telephones, fire and other alarms, etc.) and extinguishing equipment (hose reels and fire extinguishers) are visible and accessible.

Ensuring that all signs indicating smoke and fire doors, communication equipment, extinguishing equipment, escape routes and other means of escape are clearly visible.

Keeping entrances to service and kitchen lifts, laundry and refuse chutes shut.

Disposing of refuse into specially provided and safely positioned containers. Never putting hot, smouldering or burning materials into refuse chutes.

Keeping electrical installations, wiring, flexes and plugs in serviceable condition.

Keeping fume hoods of cooking equipment clean and regularly inspecting and maintaining grease traps and filters, where fitted, in a clean, serviceable condition.

Never storing any combustible materials near central heating boilers.

Monthly Inspection
Checking the capacity of the power supply and proper working of the emergency lighting plant.

Periodic Inspection
Chimneys and flues.

Ventilation ducts and fans.

Air-conditioning plant.

Heating and boiler installations.

Main electrical switchgear (to be inspected every 6 months by a qualified electrician).

Note: This is a list of suggested **additional** precautions. It does not refer to the normal essential maintenance and regular checking of all fire detection and alarm systems and fire extinguishing equipment.

Fig 8.4 Fire prevention checklist – example (Courtesy of the Hotel and Catering Training Board)

presence of maintenance contractors so that they can be accounted for in the event of a fire.

Poorly maintained electrical equipment is a common cause of fire and so flexes, cables, plugs, fuses, sockets etc. should be regularly inspected. It may be worth while instigating a checking system for residents who use their own electrical equipment such as fires, audio systems, hair care appliances etc. Students are particularly prone to overloading sockets.

Inspection of the emergency lighting system and the illumination of fire exit signs should be included in the maintenance programme.

4 Building security

Building security is put into jeopardy by poor maintenance and by dishonesty. Poor maintenance can result in locks not working or remaining faulty, and damaged windows and doors which tempt vandalism and encourage illegal entry. Efficient management and supervision of the maintenance programme should help to keep these security problems to a minimum.

Dishonesty is a much harder problem to tackle as it cannot be contained within any one department, and building maintenance will undoubtedly involve the presence of contracted-in staff whose honesty will not necessarily have been checked out. (Although reputable contractors should abide by codes of conduct if they wish to be respected in their particular trade.) The maintenance manager, therefore, should make every effort to screen his or her own staff prior to offering employment and then to reduce the number of situations where the temptation to be dishonest may be too strong to resist. There follow several examples of how security risks can be reduced:

■ Identification uniforms, badges, photo charts
■ Constantly manned doors for those which must be kept unlocked
■ Closed-circuit television
■ Alarm systems
■ Efficient and well-supervised system of locks, e.g. key books, keyless locks
■ Thorough induction and continuous training and supervision of all staff
■ Provision of individual lockers for staff, away from store areas and delivery points if possible
■ Instigation and regular monitoring of stock control systems
■ Fitting of window locks and special security button openings for fire exit doors
■ Permanent labelling of the company property, e.g. ladders, tools, furniture
■ Regular inspection of lighting, both internal and external, to avoid 'hidden' corners and entrances. Consider the use of 'movement sensitive' lights which only come on when movement within their range is detected
■ Use of anti-climb paint on drain pipes
■ Use of raised external fire escape steps
■ Good liaison between departmental heads resulting in familiarity with the 'norm'.

Maintenance programmes

The type of building, its location, clientele and complexity, provide the guidelines for setting the standard of maintenance to be achieved both internally and externally. Hospital patients, for example, are particularly vulnerable to bacteria and so dust control and periodic cleaning in patient areas have a high priority and this should be reflected in the cleaning/maintenance budget. A luxury hotel could well include leisure areas such as exercise rooms, swimming pools, saunas, sun beds, beauty salons, squash courts etc., the safety rules for which necessitate a high degree of supervision and frequent inspections. At the other end of the market, self-catering units require only occasional inspection, although an efficient system of communication is essential to cope with repairs and damage.

Control of maintenance involves:

- The creation of an inspection cycle (*see* Figs 8.5 and 8.6).
- The development of planned maintenance procedures (work cards/schedules).
- The compilation of a series of work schedules to include the above procedures and to link in with the inspection cycle.
- The structuring of supervision during cleaning and maintenance work (*see* Fig 8.7).
- The organising of post-job inspections.

Apart from the departmental managers, who should be constantly aware of the physical state of the areas for which they are responsible, the housekeeping department and maintenance department *must* work together

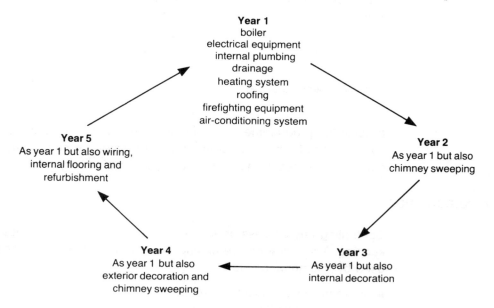

Fig 8.5 Maintenance inspection cycle (1–5 years)

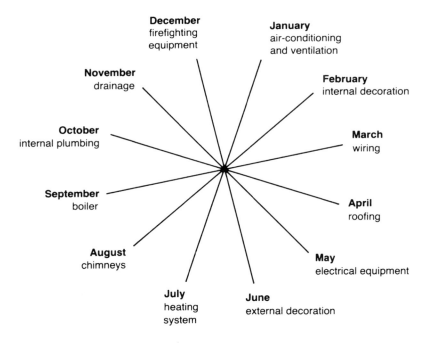

Fig 8.6 Maintenance inspection cycle (annual)

Periodic (3–6 months)	Weekly/fortnightly	Daily
deep cleaning of carpets	internal windows	linen
curtain cleaning	polishing	dusting/wiping
exterior window cleaning	lighting checks	sanitary areas
floor polish renovation	electrical appliances	kitchens
furniture cleaning	waste bins	floors
	spray buffing	
	floor scrubbing	
	damp wiping	

Fig 8.7 Cleaning cycle

to fulfill the programme of maintenance adopted when a building is commissioned. This programme must, however, be sufficiently flexible to cater for changes in facilities, staffing and technology.

Documentation

Controlling any process or series of activities inevitably necessitates record keeping. The following are examples of some of the main types of document used by maintenance staff:

- bedroom/ward inspection sheets
- public area checklists
- maintenance request forms

The following points should be considered prior to the adoption of a redecoration policy:

■ Considerable inconvenience can be suffered by staff and customers from a smell of paint, stepping over dust sheets, squeezing past ladders, the noise of workers' radios etc.
■ The environment can become very hazardous with inflammable paint, rags etc. lying around.
■ Security can be put at risk by an increase in contracted-in staff, or windows left open to allow paint fumes to escape.
■ Areas have to be closed, putting strain on the remainder of the space in the building, e.g. hospital wards.
■ Revenue is reduced as rooms are unavailable for letting.

However, there are also advantages to redecoration.

■ A well-decorated, well-maintained building helps to keep staff morale high, and is more attractive to customers.
■ Seasonal businesses can offer 'alternative work' to staff in the off-peak periods, i.e. redecorating, thus maintaining their services for the following season.
■ Standards of hygiene are maintained.
■ Frequent redecoration enables staff to get used to coping with an 'invasion' from maintenance staff, so that co-operation is more easily attained, resulting in greater efficiency.

Planning for redecoration involves the hire or purchase and subsequent storage of a number of items:

■ paint rollers/brushes/spray applicators/trays
■ buckets/steps/ladders/scaffolding/cradles
■ dust sheets/polythene sheeting
■ eye, nose and ear protectors and protective clothing
■ warning notices/barriers.

There should also be a record kept of the materials used so that reordering is straightforward and the programme can be costed accurately and measured against the budget. These details should include the make, type, shade, code number, supplier, amount used, cost per unit and assessment of quality. This information is invaluable when making decisions on refurbishment.

2 Refurbishment

Any establishment with a heavy emphasis on marketing will consider refurbishment every 3–5 years. Major refurbishment may involve suspension of the operation for a few days or even several months, and will probably involve advice from an interior designer. The internal maintenance team may have little involvement in a large programme but, depending on the size of the establishment, the maintenance manager and housekeeper should be included in the planning. It is very important that they should obtain specification details of the replaced hard surfaces, upholstery, finishes, and lighting (maximum wattages etc.) so that inventories can be altered accordingly.

Refurbishment will require the production of a revised maintenance programme and a reassessment of staffing requirements.

Maintaining the environment

1   Light

Natural light should be used whenever possible and must be retained by regular window cleaning both inside and outside, and by ensuring that curtains, blinds, plants, books and furniture are not allowed to block too much window area. Natural light can be intensified by the use of mirrors and light coloured wall surfaces which will reflect light rays.

Unless a regular programme of window cleaning takes place the inside of a building can look dull and depressing, and this creates an impression of management inefficiency. Most large buildings require a permanent team of window cleaners, employed either directly or on contract. In many cases the internal glazing is looked after by the housekeeping department.

It is important to remember that the safety of contractors is the responsibility of the company on whose premises they are working, therefore supervision of outdoor window cleaners must not be neglected: ladders must be safe and placed on even surfaces, cradles must be inspected frequently. To overcome the expense and organisation involved in employing window cleaners, pivot windows may be installed, thus enabling the inside and outside surfaces to be attended to simultaneously by housekeeping staff. These will need to be checked regularly to prevent them seizing up, especially after redecoration has occurred when paint may have found its way into the swivel joints.

Artificial light is normally used where natural lighting is inadequate. The maintenance department is responsible for ordering, storing and replacing all artificial light fittings. These can vary considerably and it is important to keep a record of the types of artificial light fittings required in each area of the building.

The efficiency of artificial light must be maintained by regular cleaning of the shades and covers which create the desired lighting effect and atmosphere. These may be made from a variety of materials such as glass, plastic or metal. The heat generated by the filament bulb or fluorescent tube can cause discoloration and the light source attracts flies and moths. Ceiling lights should be included during periodic cleaning. Those which can be lowered or which are in areas where the presence of dust can be a danger, such as hospital examination rooms, will be attended to more frequently, usually by housekeeping staff.

Department	Location

Details of maintenance required

Date of request	Requested by:

Maintenance department only

Work inspected by:	Date:

Details of work carried out

Work carried out by:	Date:

Fig 8.10 Maintenance report form – example

Liaison with the housekeeping department is essential to ensure that artificial lighting is maintained. Information regarding replacements is obtained through a maintenance report form (*see* Fig 8.10) which is completed by individual departments and passed to maintenance. Large, inaccessible light fittings may require the use of scaffolding in order to clean them or replace bulbs. This is often the case in entrance foyers where chandeliers are found. Equipment needed to maintain good lighting includes:

- scaffolding on wheels
- buckets (oblong or round)
- squeegees
- sheepskin squeegees
- scrim
- liquid detergent
- ladders
- dust sheets
- newspaper
- replacement bulbs, fluorescent tubes
- warning signs.

(There is further discussion of lighting in Chapter 5.)

2 Sound

Sounds can be defined as audible air vibrations. They must be kept under control in multi-occupancy buildings, such as those in the hospitality industry. Undesirable sounds which disturb, annoy or intrude on people's activities are referred to as noise.

Excessive noise can affect a person physically, psychologically and socially. It can make speech communication difficult so that instructions may be misunderstood; cause distraction and reduce concentration and therefore be the cause of an accident; interfere with sleep and therefore be irritating to guests, patients or residents; and at high levels cause permanent damage to hearing, even if the hearer likes the sound, e.g. discos and radios.

Noise can be generated by machinery, e.g. vacuum cleaners, food mixers, telephones, electric drills, p.a. systems, as well as by day-to-day living and working activities. It is intensified in confined spaces or if an area has predominantly non-absorbent surfaces, such as those found in kitchens and bathrooms. The problem in kitchens can be overcome by using plastic bowls, rubber bungs on the base of table legs to reduce impact sounds, and regular inspection and maintenance of ventilation systems and electrical machinery. Trolley wheels and door hinges should be oiled and staff should be instructed in the importance of working quietly, e.g. not letting doors bang, placing equipment down rather than letting it drop. Conversely all staff should be aware of the normal sounds to be heard from machinery and so be able to identify unusual noises which indicate possible danger.

a Noise measurement

Sound levels are measured in decibels (dB). It is important that all managers are aware of acceptable levels in certain areas, as excessive noise can have a debilitating effect on the workforce as well as possibly causing serious physical damage.

Recommended sound levels:

Bedroom − 25 dB

rot are buckled skirtings and cracking paintwork behind which may be found white fungal strands, large fruiting bodies or rust-coloured spore dust. To cure dry rot, it is necessary to cut away all affected timber and plaster at least 600mm beyond signs of decay, burn the wood, and spray the contaminated waste with a fungicide, together with the replacement wood. This is best left to a specialist contractor, although dry rot fluid can be purchased. Dry rot spreads more rapidly than wet rot and is likely to attack structural joists and rafters as well as window frames, skirting and floorboards. Figure 8.12 illustrates damage caused by dry rot.

b Wet rot

This is so called because its ideal conditions for growth are 40% minimum moisture content. It is commonly found in window sills and at the base of exterior doors where moisture seeps in through tiny cracks in the paintwork. This moisture is then trapped behind the paint and builds up to the point which attracts rot. Wet rot spreads less quickly than dry rot and can be cured by thorough drying of the affected area, but unless the drying out process is thorough it may give rise to the ideal conditions for dry rot development (*see* Fig 8.13).

Fig 8.13 Wet rot damage (Courtesy of Rentokil)

Exterior woodwork such as that used for barge boarding and decorative panelling is particularly vulnerable to decay and damage. Unless adequately coated with a water repellent, it will absorb water and swell then shrink, thus causing stress so that joints break and allow the entry of fungus spores. Outdoor furniture such as benches, sheds, fences, gates etc. should also be treated with an organic solvent type of wood preservative.

Regular maintenance tasks

Certain maintenance tasks cannot and need not wait for an inspection before being identified as necessary. These will be included in the work schedules of the maintenance staff and are an essential part of maintaining the building's structure and services. These include:

- Clearing drains. This is particularly important in autumn when falling leaves blow into the side of a building.
- Re-treating of exterior woodwork.
- Cleaning gutters. Again this is necessary in autumn, as well as after roofing work has been carried out and after heavy snowfalls followed by freezing.
- Checking and repairing insulation both internal, cavity wall and internal/external membranes.
- Sweeping chimneys.
- Cleaning ventilation fans, ducts, grilles and vents.
- Bleeding radiators to remove air locks.
- Replacing light bulbs and tubes before they run out.
- Stripping and re-sealing floor surfaces.
- Washing paintwork and re-decorating internally.
- Sweeping and hosing down external paved areas and leisure pool areas.
- Raking gravel, cutting grass etc.

The outside tasks will vary according to whether gardening staff are employed.

Maintaining hygiene

A safe building will usually mean it is also healthy. The Health and Safety at Work Act, the Food and Drugs Act and the Food Hygiene Regulations provide the main legislative guidance on hygiene and safety for the hospitality industry.

Although departmental managers have responsibility for the hygiene of their particular sections, the maintenance manager should have responsibility for maintaining the building fabric in a hygienic state. This will include the visible areas of the structure as well as the hidden areas, such as under floorboards, roof spaces, service ducts, drains, lift shafts etc.

Typical hygiene hazards would include:

- cracked or chipped floor and wall tiles
- damaged wiring and pipework
- prolonged unpleasant, musty smells
- excessive litter
- dirty maintenance equipment
- dark, damp, moist, warm atmospheres
- 'spoilt' foodstuffs.

To reduce these hazards it is necessary to understand how they may have arisen.

Damaged tiles occur through wear and tear but may have been caused by poor workmanship when they were laid. It may be that their quality was insufficient for the wear they received or even the wrong choice of surface for that particular area.

Damaged wiring and pipework can be created by bad weather (particularly on external downpipes), poor workmanship during installation, carelessness when using electrical equipment (flexes becoming caught under doors etc.) or rodent attack (*see* Fig 8.14).

Smells may be due to lack of ventilation, damaged or blocked drains, storage of dirty equipment, inefficient food storage and waste disposal, pest infestation, moulds and fungal growth.

Litter is due to inefficient waste disposal methods which include lack of waste disposal containers, lackadaisical staff, or inadequate training and supervision of staff.

Fig 8.14 Mouse gnawing power cable (Courtesy of Rentokil)

Dirty maintenance equipment is due to poor supervision and inadequate training. Managers may also be allowing insufficient time in work schedules for the cleaning down of equipment.

Dark, damp, moist, warm atmospheres are ideal conditions for bacteria, rodents, insects etc. to flourish. They exist in all areas of a building where ventilation and light are difficult to achieve.

Although all of these hazards are serious, waste disposal and pest infestation are probably the most prevalent in buildings used for hospitality.

1 Waste disposal

Although maintenance staff are not responsible for generating a large amount of waste, they may have a responsibility for ensuring that any waste generated is stored in a hygienic fashion and removed from the premises as soon as possible. There are several categories of waste, some more difficult and costly to remove than others.

a Construction waste

This is usually of a solid nature and includes building materials such as masonry, metal pipes, wood products such as hardboard, as well as timber shavings, plasterboard, plastic tubing etc. Such waste is usually best removed by hiring a skip or contacting the local authority cleansing department.

b Clinical waste

This may be generated in any area involved in nursing, i.e. hospitals, sanitoria, first aid rooms, convalescent homes, clinics etc. It will include items such as infected dressings, syringes, needles, often aerosol cans and a considerable amount of broken glass, not to mention diseased limbs. This type of waste can be extremely dangerous and care should be taken to ensure storage bags are sealed when full and are not punctured, with the possible risk of spread of infection. Most hospitals operate a colour code system for storage of clinical waste and sharp items are usually placed in strong cardboard containers labelled 'sharps'. Incineration is the best system for disposing of clinical waste, and should occur as soon as possible after collection. Many hospital sites have their own incineration plant (the heat from which supplements the main heating system). However, care should be taken to extract aerosol cans as they will explode under hot conditions and may cause damage to the incinerator.

c Human waste

This is dealt with by the plumbing system; therefore drains, water seals, waste stacks, bathroom fittings etc. must be regularly inspected if hygiene is to be maintained (see Chapter 4). Local authorities will undertake to empty cesspits and septic tanks but regular inspection of these systems will prevent overflowing and the subsequent health hazards which would ensue. Feminine waste products are usually disposed of under contract by 'hygiene services'.

d Dry waste

This consists of paper, cardboard, textiles, plastic cartons, glass, tins etc. These items tend to be bulky and are often sufficiently light to be blown about in windy weather. They should therefore be reduced in volume as much as possible before being removed for incineration or recycling. This can be done manually or by using a shredder or compactor.

e Wet waste or swill

This consists primarily of food waste and will include fatty substances which, if not disposed of with care, will cause blockages in the plumbing system and hazards if incineration is carried out. Food waste should be kept to a minimum by efficient catering methods but what is generated should, if possible, be put through a grinder so that it can be flushed away in the plumbing system. The use of grease traps in kitchens should be encouraged (*see* Chapter 4).

The choice of waste disposal equipment will depend on the type and amount of waste generated by the activities carried out in the building, therefore discussions on this take place when planning a building. Typical supplies, equipment and systems which will need maintaining are:

■ bags ■ bins ■ conveyors ■ carts ■ chutes ■ compactors ■ shredders ■ grinders ■ incinerators ■ pulpers

All these items and the areas in which they operate must be kept in a hygienic condition. This will involve regular cleaning of bag holders and lids (internal and external); sweeping and hosing down of waste collection points; frequent inspection of waste chutes to prevent blockages which in turn can be a fire hazard; steam cleaning of areas where waste becomes too difficult to remove by sweeping, wiping or hosing down.

It is advisable to use sanitising agents such as disinfectants periodically, but these are only truly effective on clean surfaces and may be ineffective when the following substances are present: blood, vomit, urine, faeces, milk, hard water, cotton wool, paper, rubber, wood, cork. It is also important to ensure that detergents used around food storage, preparation and service areas are those often described as sanitising agents or QUATS (quarternary ammonium compounds) as they have no apparent taste or smell.

2 Pest control (insects and rodents)

Inefficient waste disposal routines will inevitably create ideal conditions for certain pests. Pests carry diseases and can cause not only numerous types of food poisoning but also typhus, typhoid, encephalitis, malaria and even bubonic plague. They require water, food and a place to breed which is dark, warm and undisturbed, to survive.

It is obviously impossible to eliminate moisture from external areas, but internal areas should be kept as dry as possible. Spillages must be cleared immediately, leaking pipes and dripping taps reported and repaired as soon as possible, and condensation reduced to a minimum.

Food can be found in ordinary dust particles, therefore basic cleanliness will go a long way to reducing food availability, but many pests are attracted to specific substances.

a Rodents (rats, mice, squirrels, hedgehogs, voles)

Rats and mice are the most prevalent rodents in buildings used in the hospitality industry. They are 'gnawing' animals and can cause considerable damage to a building structure and its services. It is not unknown for rats or mice to eat through electric cables causing short circuits and therefore creating a fire hazard (see Fig 8.14). They can also damage gas and water mains.

The effect of rats on foodstuffs is one of destruction rather than consumption. They foul vast quantities with urine and droppings and unless their presence is detected, food poisoning will result or the unnecessary expense of replacement will be incurred. Mice, however, are attracted particularly to chocolate, nuts, seeds and cereals.

Rodents have a very acute sense of smell, can climb easily and can squeeze through very small gaps. They nest in deposits of paper and packaging and so a build-up of such items should be avoided. The control of rodents can only occur by blocking all possible entry holes, e.g. gaps around pipework and removing all food sources, e.g. clearing spillages and covering waste bins. Baits should be strategically placed near signs of infestation and monitored. Many establishments employ a contractor, such as Rentokil, to eradicate rodents and implement a system whereby infestation can be monitored. These contractors should belong to the British Pest Control Association and all staff should be encouraged to co-operate with them by keeping bait boxes in position and reporting any signs of rodent habitation (droppings, black smears, gnaw marks, scuttling sounds).

b Cats, dogs and birds

These animals should be discouraged from entering buildings and indeed from entering the grounds. They shed fur and feathers and spread bacteria. Birds, especially starlings, can cause considerable deterioration to the exterior of a building as well as making it look unsightly. They can enter roof spaces in which bacteria can breed and eventually penetrate the building below. Cats and dogs may carry fleas in their fur and tread in dirt and dust, which unless removed will attract insects.

c Insects

Figure 8.5 listing insect detection and control identifies the most common insects to be found inside buildings and how they can be controlled. Spiders and mites are not included in this list as they are not strictly insects. Their

Pest detection and control

Insect	Typical food sources	Detection	Control procedures
Bed bugs	Human blood	Unpleasant smell Reports of bites on humans (small, hard, white swellings)	Bedroom hygiene, especially maintenance of plaster, wallpaper, wooden furniture Lindane spray Professionally applied insecticide
Carpet beetle	Feathers, fur, wool, skinflakes, hair	Irregular holes in the seams of textile fabrics, especially wool	Inspection of roof eaves for dead birds Inspection of pipe lagging Cleanliness of shelves, floorboards, cupboards, carpets, upholstery, mothproofing Use Lindane or Cabary insect powder under carpets and in crevices Use moth repellent crystals around stored clothes, blankets, etc
Cockroaches	Most types of foodstuffs	Food spoilage, unpleasant smell, food poisoning outbreak; visual detection	Use insecticide spray in floor cavities, pipe runs, sink areas Use professionally applied baits/powders
Fleas	Fur, feathers, organic debris, fluff, dust	Irritating bites causing small, red spots; visual detection	Burn infested bedding Prevent entry of cats, dogs, birds Check for birds' nests internally and on building exterior Use insecticide spray on bed frames and floor surfaces
Furniture beetle	Unprotected wood	Clean round holes in wooden furniture, joists, rafters, floorboards, packing cases	Inject holes with woodworm killer, then coat infested areas Use insecticidal polish
Flies	Decaying organic matter, refuse	Reports of diarrhoea, dysentery, diphtheria and gastro-enteritis can all indicate food contamination by flies	Promptly dispose of food waste, tins, bottles, jars Efficient control of refuse storage Fly screens fitted over opening windows
Lice	Human blood, hair, textile fibres	Reports of bites, often on scalp, constant scratching	Personal hygiene Bedroom hygiene Thorough cleaning
Moths	Soiled, coloured wool, leather, dried fruit, cork	Holes in textile fabrics Spoilage of dried fruit	Thorough cleaning Store textiles and leather in sealed bags in cool areas Use naphthalene tablets in linen rooms Mothproof carpets and upholstery
Silverfish	Carbonate material such as wallpaper paste, adhesives	Damage to wallpaper, books, furniture (if glued together)	Efficient maintenance and insulation of the plumbing system Use of Carbrary insect powder in cracks around plumbing fittings

Fig 8.15   Pest detection and control

presence however is an indication of the need to improve hygiene standards. They may also cause revulsion in some people and deter staff from working in areas where they have been seen. Spiders do, in fact, destroy other insects which cause damage. Dust mites may also cause an allergic reaction in people coming into contact with them, for example asthmatics.

Maintenance equipment

Whatever method is used to obtain equipment it is important to ensure that adequate safe storage space is made available and that each item is itself kept clean and in a safe condition. Use and care of equipment should be an essential part of an induction programme for employees with back-up training sessions when new equipment is purchased.

Equipment belonging to the maintenance department is likely to be found in several areas of a building, both inside and outside. It is therefore very important to keep a record of where it is at any one time, so that when the work for which it is needed is completed, it is returned to its storage area.

An inventory should also be kept detailing the following information for each group of items in stock:

- purchase date
- supplier
- price
- servicing recommendations
- maintenance instructions
- guarantee period
- local agent
- repairs carried out
- cost of repairs carried out

1 Typical maintenance equipment

Equipment used by maintenance staff is often of a specialised nature and so may be hired; this reduces capital expenditure and eliminates the need for safe storage, e.g. shampooing machines, sanders, high pressure washers, scaffolding towers, suspended platforms and cradles. Items such as cloths, mops, brushes, vacuums, scrubbers and polishers will be used more frequently by the housekeeping staff, but the following pieces of equipment will receive frequent use by maintenance staff.

a Squeegees

These are used to remove liquids from large, even, flat surfaces such as glass, floor and wall areas. They consist of a rubber strip attached to a metal holder and a handle. Both the rubber strip and the handle can vary in width and length.

5   Replacement

This policy is related to that for depreciation. Once an item of equipment or furniture has reached the end of its period of useful life, there is an option to buy new or keep it going, with the possibility of increased maintenance costs or break-down. A good maintenance manager should keep up to date with his/her knowledge of models, systems and costs. Before replacing plant and equipment a specification of what is required must be prepared (*see* Fig 8.16). This will be sent to potential suppliers so they can tender for the order.

It may be that after obtaining at least three quotes, the company will decide not to replace but to compromise by hiring or leasing, both of which have advantages and disadvantages depending on the existing number and skills of establishment staff, the number of items required and the terms of the lease/hire/rent agreement negotiated.

a   Leasing

This is an arrangement whereby the lessee (borrower) has the use of a specific item on payment of a specified sum of money over an agreed period. The lessor retains ownership. The borrowers choose the specific item they wish to lease, thus enabling them to acquire the use of expensive equipment such as computers, floor maintenance equipment, scaffolding towers and so on by paying for it out of revenue expenditure, not capital expenditure. The amount is fixed for the duration of the lease agreement.

b   Hiring and renting

A hire company purchases the items it wishes to hire out prior to being approached by a borrower. The borrower can therefore only hire from the stock held by the hire company. It should be possible to update the equipment although the amount of rent may increase. Hiring can be for an indefinite period.

Exercises

1   Carry out a life cycle costing exercise on one part of a building with which you are familiar.

2   Ascertain the safety policy of a hospitality outlet and check that it is being followed.

3   Assess the work required by the maintenance division of a hospitality outlet, then:
   a design a labour structure
   b cost it out
   c develop a control and supervision system for monitoring staff performance.

4   Assess the equipment requirements of a typical hospitality unit. Investigate the actual equipment provision and report on your findings, offering recommendations for improvement in the amount, allocation, storage, maintenance, etc. of equipment.

5   Choose a front of house and back of house area. Describe in detail the maintenance requirements of the housekeeping and maintenance departments in both the long term and short term.

9 Leisure, health and fitness areas

Objectives

After reading this chapter you should:

- Know the responsibilities of staff involved in the operation of a leisure complex.
- Be aware of the need for constant maintenance of leisure equipment and facilities.
- Understand the importance of correctly maintained chemical solutions in swimming/leisure pools.
- Have an appreciation of the safety requirements and procedures necessary for the legal operation of leisure/health/fitness areas.

Introduction

No publication on hospitality would be complete without reference to leisure or recreational facilities. These usually include one or more of the following:

swimming pools/whirlpools
saunas
sunbeds
multigyms
squash courts
indoor games areas

Such areas may be designed and built at the same time as the main building complex but many are created from existing buildings or added either as an extension or a separate annexe. The latter has advantages in that non-residents can use the facilities without encroaching on the residents' areas. In fact, the high capital and maintenance costs make it necessary for most hotels to offer membership to non-residents, despite the problems of availability and security thus created.

Staffing

The addition of a leisure area to a residential building such as a hotel can create many problems with which the manager may be unfamiliar. It is therefore advisable that some cost be set aside in the planning stage for training in leisure management. In small establishments the manager should attend a course related to the facilities for which he or she is responsible. In a more complex situation, it may be necessary to employ a leisure manager, who should be fully conversant with the legislation, safety, hygiene and maintenance aspects of the recreational facilities. Figure 9.1 illustrates a typical staffing structure for a leisure complex.

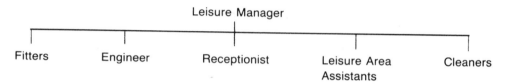

Fig 9.1 Typical staffing structure of a leisure complex

1   Leisure manager

Ideally leisure managers should have undertaken a specialist course and gained a qualification from the Institute of Baths and Recreation Management. They should also be familiar with the type of operation in which the leisure area is located, e.g. hotel or hostel management. The leisure manager should be credited with similar status to that of all other departmental managers such as restaurant manager, catering manager, banqueting manager, etc. Responsibilities include:

- personnel management
- maintenance of surfaces and plant (daily, periodic)
- control of swimming pool chemicals
- subscriptions/charges/membership
- provision and maintenance of sports equipment
- equipment hire
- provision and maintenance of towels, robes etc.
- safety and security of leisure facilities
- energy conservation
- training of leisure area operatives.

2   Leisure area assistants

These staff should all be qualified in basic first aid and, if there is a swimming pool, should have a Royal Life Saving Society's General Bronze

Public safety	Equipment and maintenance
Safety of bathers	Water testing equipment
Lifesaving	Testing of lifesaving equipment
Emergency procedures	Teaching aids
Accident and first aid procedures	Cleaning equipment
Hygiene	Cleaning agents
Staff training	Chemicals
	Pool covers
Staff safety	Filtration
Health and Safety at Work Act	Café
General safety	Bar
Emergency procedures	Oxygen equipment and resuscitator
Accidents and first aid	Gas mask
Uniform and protective clothing	Protective clothing
Discipline	Locker system
Staff training	
	General duties
Public relations	Cleaning
General principles	Water testing
Safety	Sports changeovers
Courtesy	Bar/Café
Uniform	Security
Teaching duties	Teaching/Coaching
Teaching qualifications	Lifting and moving
Swimming teaching	
Sports coaching	
Health and Safety at Work	

Fig 9.2 Leisure area assistants training programme checklist

Medallion as a minimum, and preferably have attended a plant operator's course. Their duties should include pool-side supervision, some cleaning (changing rooms), minor maintenance tasks e.g. painting and plant maintenance such as sunbed testing, backwashing of pool filters, pool testing (*see* Fig 9.2).

3 Engineer

This person will probably be employed for the whole building and would undertake more of a trouble-shooting role. In small establishments, engineers will probably be contracted-in when required. They will be consulted when problems occur with plant and machinery.

4 Receptionist

Receptionists are only required in large establishments and where the facilities are open to the public. They monitor the availability of each area,

- wave machine openings, sumps, inlets and outlets of the pool water circulation system should have protective covers or grilles and be designed in such a way that limbs cannot get trapped. Undue suction should be avoided at the opening position to prevent a body being held against the grille
- grab handles should be recessed or placed far enough from the tank wall to avoid limbs becoming trapped
- water depth should be marked clearly in both the shallow and deep ends
- diving areas must be clearly indicated
- all signs should comply with the Safety Signs Regulations 1980. Pictorial signs are recommended, supplemented with text as necessary.

Control of swimming facilities

1 Environmental conditions

Having a correct relationship between these services is vital not only to the safety and hygiene of a swimming pool area but also to the comfort of guests and staff. Excess humidity, for instance, can corrode finishes and cause electrical hazards.

a Heating

The temperature of water in a pool should not be more than 27°C. Air temperature in a pool area should be kept to 10°C above that of the water. This ratio should keep condensation to a minimum. The heating plant, fuel storage and delivery systems should be inspected and tested regularly and be included in the maintenance programme for the whole building. Steam boilers and plant must be maintained to the standards required by sections 32–35 of the Factories Act 1961.

b Ventilation

Ventilation should be draught-free. Natural ventilation should if possible be used in conjunction with air conditioning. Humidity and air movement should be balanced to maintain comfortable conditions, therefore the manager should be conversant with the air conditioning system and its controls.

c Lighting

Where natural lighting is provided the glare of the water can become irritating to pool users; therefore blinds, screens or tinted glass should be used. Where artificial lighting is used, fittings should be suitably covered and sealed against moisture ingress and corrosion from contaminants in the atmosphere. Emergency lighting should be tested daily and suspended light fittings every six months.

The wet, corrosive atmosphere in a swimming pool area magnifies the risks from electricity. The following British Standard Numbers refer to the safety of specific electrical installations: BS 5305/4343/5490/4293/3535.

2 Swimming pool water treatment

Water treatment requires the use of chemicals. The leisure manager should ensure that they are handled correctly from delivery to their mix with water. The following points highlight areas of concern:

a Delivery

- Newly delivered chemicals should never be left unattended.
- Pipework for bulk deliveries should be easily identifiable by the use of different pipework, fittings, colours etc.
- Every item must be clearly labelled. (Packaging and labelling of Dangerous Substances Regulations 1984.)

b Storage

- All storage areas should be clearly marked and situated in a secure location.
- Ground floor storage is advisable to assist in ventilation as well as movement of cylinders etc but storage should be away from public entrances, windows and ventilation intakes.
- Containers must be kept away from direct sunlight and hot pipes.
- Dry goods should be raised from the ground in case of leakage from the pool area.
- Incompatible materials should be stored in separate areas, e.g. acids/alkalis.
- Staff involved in movement of chemicals, whether for storage, dilution, mixing or maintenance, should have access to the following items: impervious boots, impervious aprons, impervious gauntlets, eye protection, respiratory protection.

c Spillages

These should be dealt with as soon as possible and precautions made to prevent any chemicals entering a drain, unless arrangements have been made with the water authority. There should be a written emergency procedure for dealing with any major leakage of toxic gas. This should include an evacuation procedure for the whole site.

d Chemical composition of pool water

Swimming pools should always be visually attractive, comfortable to swim in and safe from any risk of the spread of infectious disease. The water should therefore be clear, warm and sterile. This is achieved by 'water balance', i.e. the relationship between:

pH/chlorine
alkalinity
calcium hardness
total dissolved solids (TDS)
temperature

Water balance can only be achieved by regular, frequent testing and sampling of the water.

Chlorine

Chlorine is available in two parts: free and residual (a little like milk being made up of curds and whey). *Free chlorine* kills off bacteria but tends to burn off all dead skin, hair, fats and cosmetics, *residual chlorine* has little effect on bacteria. It is the relationship between free and residual which is important. Too little free chlorine can result in unpleasant odours and eye irritation. The tests for chlorine content of the water should measure both free chlorine and residual chlorine. Typical measurements would be:

> 1.0 free chlorine/1.5 total residual chlorine

To calculate the *combined chlorine* content the free chlorine measurement should be deducted from that for total residual chlorine, i.e. $1.5 - 1.0 = 0.5$. The combined chlorine measurement should be kept as low as possible. Chlorine should be tested several times each day.

pH

This should be kept between 7.2 and 7.8. (The pH of eyes is about 7.2.) If pH is too high, the water can become cloudy and reduce the efficiency of free chlorine. pH can be lowered by using sodium bisulphate. If pH is too low, damage can be caused to pipeline valves and grouting, and it can cause irritation to the eyes, ears, nose and throat. pH can be increased using sodium carbonate. Tests should be carried out throughout the day.

Alkalinity

This should be kept between 150 and 200mg:1. If it is too low, pH will be difficult to control, corrosion will occur to pipes etc, and conditions will seem uncomfortable for bathers. The addition of sodium bicarbonate will increase alkalinity. If alkalinity is too high, water will become cloudy and corrosion will occur but pH cannot be adjusted. To lower alkalinity, a weak solution of dry acid should be added. Alkalinity should be tested weekly.

Calcium hardness

This indicates the mineral content. High levels are not detrimental but an acceptable range is 200–250mg:1. Dilution will reduce hardness. Tests should be carried out weekly.

Total dissolved solids

This includes everything which is added to the pool and not removed by either filters or evolved from the water as a gas. High readings cause extensive corrosion; a reduction can be made by dilution.

Leisure managers should rota the staff so that they all carry out tests. Charts indicating test procedures should be clear and available for reference.

Any adverse pool conditions should be notified to the manager immediately (*see* Figs 9.5 and 9.6).

Prevention

Sodium Hypochlorite (12/15% available chlorine) is recommended as a pool disinfectant. The gas must stay in solution form. It will not do so if there is a change in temperature or if a chemical reaction occurs. To ensure this does not happen the disinfectant must be handled with care:

- wear the protective rubber clothing provided
- do not lift the containers above waist high
- do not mix the disinfectant with anything except water

If chlorine gas is detected:

1 Evacuate the area in the same way as if there were a fire. Unlike smoke, however, chlorine gas is heavy – therefore it would be dangerous to keep low down.

2 Breathing apparatus must be available for use while awaiting the fire brigade.

Fig 9.5 Chlorine leakage procedure

Suggested chemical cleaning procedures

1 Fill carboy with 9 litres of hypo, using a funnel and appropriate safety equipment.

2 Transport hypo to area of use in the carboy.

3 Fill carboy with tapwater.

4 Apply hypo solution to the floor area using plastic watering can.

5 Spread out solution using deck scrubber to loosen dirt.

6 Leave for 5 minutes.

7 Deck scrub total floor surface.

8 Hose down floor surface, ensuring that no chemical remains on the floor, or in any gulleys.

9 Return all equipment to store/plant room.

Slackness in carrying out the procedure outlined above is likely to cause distress to users of the pool areas and would be in contravention of the Health and Safety at Work Act.

CHEMICALS CAN CAUSE INJURY – ACT RESPONSIBLY AND SAFELY

Fig 9.6 Suggested chemical cleaning procedure